THE
TRUTH
HAS
CHANGED

JOSH FOX

INTRODUCTION BY **BILL McKIBBEN**

SEVEN STORIES PRESS NEW YORK · OAKLAND · LONDON

SEVEN STORIES PRESS
140 Watts Street
New York, NY 10013
sevenstories.com

College professors and high school and middle school
teachers may order free examination copies of Seven Stories Press titles.
To order, visit www.sevenstories.com
or send a fax on school letterhead to (212) 226-1411.

LIBRARY OF CONGRESS CATALOGING-IN-PUBLICATION DATA
Names: Fox, Josh, 1972- author.
Title: The truth has changed / Josh Fox.
Description: First edition. | New York : Seven Stories Press, [2018]
Identifiers: LCCN 2018017399| ISBN 9781609809232 (pbk.) | ISBN
9781609809249 (ebook)
Subjects: LCSH: Political culture--United States. | Truth--Political
aspects--United States. | Climatic changes--Political aspects--United
States. | United States--Environmental conditions--Political aspects. |
United States--Politics and government--21st century.
Classification: LCC JK1726 .F656 2018 | DDC 306.20973--dc23
LC record available at https://lccn.loc.gov/2018017399]

Printed in the USA.

9 8 7 6 5 4 3 2 1

PHOTO CREDITS

p. 10 & 12: © 2001 The Associated Press. Reprinted by permission.
p. 108: © 2011 Getty Images. Reprinted by permission.
All other photos courtesy of the author.

DEDICATED TO THE MEMORY OF
Manuel Lutgenhorst, Joe Frank,
and of course, Spalding Gray

CONTENTS

PART TWO

FOREWORD

BILL McKIBBEN

Josh Fox is a remarkable human being, and this is a remarkable document, bringing together his many lives: artist, truth teller, campaigner. These are not, it turns out, different tasks. They're the same job, on different days.

Mostly the world got to know Josh through *GASLAND*, his documentary account of the fracking boom across America. Back before most people knew it was going on, and certainly before most people sensed any trouble, Josh had traveled to the rural margins of an increasingly urban and suburban nation, and brought back the goods: the science about what happened when you blew apart the subsurface geology to get at gas, but also the picture of what happened to communities, and to individual lives. And he brought back the clip: of a man lighting his faucet on fire. That moment summed up an entire technology—indeed, an entire careless greedy approach to the world around us.

That he had struck a nerve was obvious—the reaction from the oil and gas industry was immediate and overwhelming: Orwellian "truth squads" to try and cover up the facts, constant campaigns of harassment, expensive efforts to silence him and his colleagues. Believe me, this kind of pressure is hard to endure. But he's been able to—indeed, over time it may have freed him to act with a kind of compassion and conviction that goes beyond even the normal realm of the documentarian.

Wherever people are trying to stand up to the power of the fossil fuel industry, that's where he's been. In Louisiana, where new gas plants and oil pipelines are under siege. At Standing Rock, in the ultimate confrontation with the naked power of the world's richest industry. In the Caribbean after Maria, where the full strength of a warmed ocean had been on display. He's always got his camera (at a memorable protest outside the world's largest coal port in Australia, he managed to flip it to a friend in a neighboring boat just as the police craft rammed into his vessel). But he's also always got his wits about him—the artistic sense that served him well in his years as a director, and that has allowed him to tell the stories he now witnesses in a vernacular that can and does penetrate.

Not many Americans have seen as much as Josh Fox has in recent years—not many white Americans, anyway. And you could forgive him if he'd turned bitter, turned in on himself. It is noteworthy, and even noble, that he has taken the opposite tack, becoming ever more immersed in the hurly-burly of our political life. In the time of Trump, that's no small gift to the Republic, for we need people with his slashing ability to communicate across the sea of idiocy that threatens to numb us all. Art is for breaking through numbness, and Josh Fox is an artist above all. That his art flows from fact, from science, from study makes it not dry and academic but immediate and desperate and necessary.

"THE CONDITION
OF TRUTH IS ALWAYS
TO ALLOW SUFFERING
TO SPEAK!"

—DR. CORNEL WEST

"THERE IS
NO INEVITABILITY
AS LONG AS THERE IS
A WILLINGNESS TO
CONTEMPLATE WHAT
IS HAPPENING"

—MARSHALL McLUHAN

PART ONE

The Stage is bare except for a small desk, center. Water projection screens rigged in nine positions all around the stage. When all the water screens are turned on at once it is as if the stage is raining.

PROLOGUE

Rain and windshield wipers.

How do we know what's true?

Josh raises his hand, like a student asking a question.

2012.

Interstate 95. In the car, the question is going over and over in my mind, like the windshield wipers clicking back and forth. It's coming on nightfall, and the winds are picking up. It feels like it's 3 a.m. Somehow it always feels like it's 3 a.m.

I'm on tour, speaking with students about my films, and I can't get one student's question out of my mind. Her hand was the first up at the end of the film. "How do we know what's true?" She's a senior at Sweet Briar College in Virginia, located on an old-fashioned plantation, left over from the Civil War. It's an all-female college with an equine studies program. The cost of tuition is over $50,000 a year. The students here are so wealthy that they have their own horses. They ride to their classes.

"You say all of these things about how fracking is bad and climate change is real, but then we read on the Internet that all the opposite of those things are true. So how do we know?" These kids have every possible resource at their disposal; every resource, it seems, except a mechanism for knowing what's true.

I begin to answer, when I realize that I can't properly answer this question, or at least not quickly.

It's been a long travel week, across southern states: Louisiana, Arkansas, Tennessee.

I'm trying to make it home, but it's dark, my eyes are blurry, and I am somewhere in that liminal no-man's-land that could be Maryland, could be Delaware, southern New Jersey, I've lost track. No sleep till Brooklyn.

There's a break in the rain; I gotta pull over.

AMERICAN OWNED AND OPERATED

I'm driving a ridiculous bright red rental, made by Ford, looks like it was made for a cheesy video game. It squeals a sigh of relief as I pull into a place called the Midway Motel. I stop in the parking lot because it's such a dingy, run-down, strange-looking place. One of the bands of the storm has passed over, a brief respite. But you can see from the full moon: clouds are brewing and gathering on the horizon. Big clouds, dangerous-looking clouds.

The sign out front says "American Owned And Operated. Truck Parking Available." The lights are dim, and there are three scraggly figures on the second-floor balcony, looking out at this weird, brand-new, Sonic-the-Hedgehog car that's just pulled in. I feel like I have just interrupted a drug deal, or a domestic spat, maybe both. I decide it's okay to stay, turn off the headlights, and walk toward the office.

One of the three vapors mixing with the mist in the air comes down, she's holding three bun-less hot dogs in her hand. And she says, "What can I do for you, honey?" I say, "Do you have a room?" She says, "Yes, we do. And please ignore the hot dogs. They were in the trash in room 237, perfectly good. They're for my Dobermans." As we go into the office—which has a big, bright neon sign over the door that just says "YES"—she tells me, "It's fifty-nine dollars, or sixty-four and change after tax."

She has a warm face. Wearing a low-cut pink shirt with a black push-up bra underneath. And she has no front teeth. She just has this one, disturbing stump that she's learned to cover over with her upper lip. She says, "*Hiccup, hiccup*, well, if I, *hiccup*, if I could only stop, *hiccup*, stop hiccuping, *hiccup*, I'd give you this card to fill out."

So I say, "Do you want to know the best hiccup

cure known to humanity?" And she looks at me like, "Please." So I say, "Close your eyes."

She does. I guess she's already judged me as harmless. And I say, "Take a deep breath. Hold it as long as you can. And think of something that cannot possibly exist, not even in your own mind."

She exhales and looks at me, shocked.

I say, "Works every time. Works every time. Now, you can do that anytime you want, anytime you need."

She says, "Thank you—" *Ksshhh!* The first lightning bolt hits over the side of the hill.

She says, "You know, that was easy. You know what I thought of? I thought of a day off. That can't possibly exist, not even in my own mind. It's been a year that I worked here, and I only had maybe two days off."

And my mind says to me, "Was it her husband who knocked out those front teeth? Or crystal meth? Or the economy?"

Then all of a sudden her Dobermans come bursting out of the adjoining apartment, tails wagging. She doesn't give the hot dogs to them.

"American owned and operated."

What is it that Americans who own and operate their own businesses are in for these days?

The first pitter-patter of rain on the roof starts dancing above my head. What is it that America is in for?

"Don't forget that hiccup cure. Works every time." She hands me my towels, and we both run as the downpour opens up.

The room is clean. I pull down the sheets to make sure there are no fleas, a trick that I learned in India. And I realize there's no art on the walls, and that the bathroom looks like a prison, or a camp—cinder block walls and no cups. I don't mind. Three flies have been smashed against the wall, one of them bloody. Somebody minded that.

But this place isn't so bad. It's not hiding anything. Not like the Renaissance Marriott in Nashville for $339 a night and no way to open the fucking windows. This place is telling me the truth. Truth works every time, provided, of course, you know what the truth is.

I step out on the balcony and realize, this isn't normal rain.

Sheets of water coming down in torrents, one after the other. The parking lot is glistening; you can actually see the waves of rain undulating like an ocean over the black asphalt. Trees are bending back and forth in the wind.

The motel starts to shake back and forth a little bit. I close the door, open a pretty good bottle of rye, have a quick shot, and open up my browser.

Just why does that hiccup cure work every time?

No mention of it on the Internet.

Down a rabbit hole and I am reading about evolution.

Apparently,
evolution created a microbe that
lives inside the brain of an ant.
The microbe can only reproduce
inside the stomach of a cow.
So the microbe makes the ant go mad.
The ant, possessed by a force unknown to it,
abandons its tribe,
leaves its normal pattern,
and begins to climb a blade of grass over and over.
The microbe takes over the ant's tiny brain,
and says climb climb climb—
The ant loses all of its protective survival instincts.
And eventually a cow comes along,
eats the ant,
returning the microbe to its
primal orgy grounds.
It reproduces itself,
gets shit out,
ants eat the shit.
And the cycle starts all over again.
The microbe
got inside the brain of the ant
to use it
for a purpose that the ant cannot conceive.
Climb up the blade of grass over and over
until it is destroyed—

The room violently shakes as a blast of wind hits it, snapping me out of my trance. How long have I been online?

I walk to the balcony and watch my Sonic-the-Hedgehog car flooding down the side of the hill. A torrent of muddy water is washing it away to an insurance formality.

I run to the TV.

Battery Park, lower Manhattan, is underwater. A crew reporting from Brooklyn shows the transformer at Fourteenth Street explode and all of lower Manhattan goes pitch black.

I remember the last time I was down there.

The wind is really picking up. I don't like the sound of this.

The door flies open, smashes against the hinges, and breaks, flapping in the wind. Rain is coming into the room. I head into the bathroom as the walls start to shake.

I crouch down in the bathtub and hope the roof is on solid. Wind and rain batter away. I take the top off the toilet tank and hold it over my head like a make-shift shield.

How the hell did I get here??

I really wish I had a hot dog.

Water projection screens turn on all over the stage. Images of Hurricane Sandy battering the East Coast and torrents

of rain. All of a sudden the theme from
"Singin' in the Rain" comes on loudly.
Josh begins dancing and jumping through
the projections all over the stage, getting
wet and having a great time. The dance
sequence lasts for one to two minutes. Josh
ends his dance standing on top of his desk
facing upstage.

We hear an incredibly loud sound of a jet
plane careening through the theater, erasing
the music.

The last time there wasn't a cloud in the sky.

CHURCH OF POMPEII

A huge explosion, then fade to the destroyed facade of the World Trade Center on the morning of September 12, 2001—the projections are huge, almost as if Josh is standing in the middle of the wreckage.

On the morning of 9/11, I woke up to Ryan Edwards's stenographic report.

"Wake up. They've flown planes into the World Trade Center. Both towers have collapsed."

The person I knew who was closest to the World Trade Center was Patrick McCaffrey. He worked directly underneath the buildings. But as it turned out, he had the night shift, and he got off at eight in the morning. When he finally woke up at four that afternoon I got him on the phone and he said, "Josh. They blew up my job. I hated that job. But I didn't want them to blow it up."

We slept six to a bed that night: me, my girlfriend, four of our friends, actors in my theater company, six on a hide-a-bed, pull-out sofa, like innocent children. With the TV on all night.

We'd lost something fundamental, like an amputation. "Will New York ever be New York again?" The skyline looks unexceptional, emasculated, ordinary. Like San Diego. Because, to be honest, you know, most New Yorkers just owned the *outside* of the World Trade Center. You know, that incredible shape, like two exclamation points at the end of a very long statement. But inside, inside the World Trade Center, that was something different.

I know, because I worked there.

I was a gardener, for a commercial gardening company. I took care of plants on the twenty-second, forty-first, and thirty-seventh floors, and I hated going there. I mean, we all hated going there, two or three times a week. We used to call it the "Death Star."

And I had a little watering can underneath one of the
sinks in one of the major hedge funds. And I'd go and
water all the plants. And plants in there would die,
like you've never seen plants die before in your life.
They would put them on top of an air-conditioning
vent, tropical plants, be screaming into the phone, you
know, angry, frustrated, capitalism, and look at me
when I walked in and say, "Why the hell is that plant
dying?!" And I said, "Because you're screaming at it all
day, and it belongs in a tropical island, and . . ." No, I
wouldn't say that. I would just say, "That's okay. We'll
take it away. We'll get you a new one." See, that was
the economy; the economy is predicated on rich people
throwing things away that they don't want anymore.

Or the receptionist next to the bank of elevators,
with a giant, beautiful flowering tree that had somehow dropped all of its flowers, running up to me with
the long-suffering look of the grad-school actor turned
hedge-fund temp. "I don't know what's wrong with it."
And I wanted to say, "Get out of here. You've dropped
all your flowers too."

I wonder if she survived.

And naïve little me, in my gardening greens, cried,
for my beloved country, those islands known as New
York City, which for me was a place of diversity, immigration, culture, hip-hop, punk rock, a place where all
these amazing art forms were being born, all of us on a
ship, sinking, like Spalding Gray used to say, "an island
off the coast of America." Here we are, being targeted

by insane, intolerant, religious, suicidal wackos on the other side of the planet, as if somehow we were responsible for their misery. Were we?

So the next night, on the twelfth, I get a phone call, from Aaron Unger, the Miami Jew marathon runner turned manic insomniac actor. His cousin had organized an all-night food drive for the first responders; could we be the first responders to the first responders? We were all-night people, theater people; could we come help? He said, "Report to someplace called the Church of Our Lady of Pompeii on Sixth Ave."

Down in the basement, we're making phone calls to restaurants in the phone book, asking them to donate. "We're going to go give food to the firemen; we're going to give food to the police; we're going to go give food to the first responders." "Is this legit?" "Yes, yes; it's the Church of Pompeii." They would say things like, "Oh, well, we can donate fifty duck breast sandwiches." I mean, this wasn't the Red Cross; it wasn't like white bread with yellow cheese on it. This was lower Manhattan. "We can donate forty plates of arugula with a garlic aioli." Sounds great, can we get that to go, what's your special?

We went across the street, to Joe's Pizza, the best pizza place on the face of the earth, and they just piled our carts high. We had hand trucks piled high with pizzas. We had spray-painted a sheet and put it up on the side of this hand truck that said "Church of Pompeii." Because "church" was legit, and "Pompeii" was ironic. And that felt just right.

Directly across from the church, there's the cheer-leading squad, a group of people who sat there all night, surrounded by flickering votive candles, half applause track, half vigil. Garbage trucks going by—applause. Construction trucks—applause. Bulldozers—applause. Fire trucks—huge applause. Screaming, cheering, every-thing that went by.

And walking on Sixth Avenue, at 3 a.m., the air was like television static. Thick, dusty, viscous. With our carts piled high, we head out toward the Pitt Street Fire Station, down on Delancey. Four of us, Aaron, Connie Hall, Sophie Amieva, and myself, wading in concrete dust up to our knees, which is sort of like the consis-tency of dry papier-mâché, shredded, and you realize that this was the building. This was the pulverized building; this was the dust; and in this dust was bones, and burned office furniture, paintings, plants, people.

If the wind changed, you could smell the acrid smoke, the sulfur, like burning polyester carpet, like burning plastic. It burned in your nostrils and throat, and you sensed that you should not be breathing this.

Charred sheets of paper rained down on the streets for days afterward. I grabbed a burning memo out of the air. It was on fire. I shook it out. On top, it said, in quotes: "The Rules Have Changed. Bloomberg dot com."

I had a good respirator mask, thankfully, or else I might be dead. Other folks that I know who volun-teered down there died of lung scarring, or got vicious cancers that ripped through their bodies. The EPA, on orders from the Bush administration, had told people, "Go shopping downtown." They said, "Go back to your apartments; it's all okay." They trusted them. And they died.

But we had respirator masks because we had been working on a play, a play called *The Bomb*, ten days before 9/11. A postapocalyptic vision of the future. And I had gone to Home Depot with our measly little budget, and bought six or seven good-quality respirator masks because they looked cool, and they looked scary. And here we are, going down the streets of New York City, wearing our Armageddon theater costumes. And they saved our lives.

We walked all the way downtown, turned right, made it to Pitt Street. Outside the station, there's a fireman, who comes up to us. He goes, "Don't go in there."

"But we have pizza. We have Joe's!"

He says, "We got plenty of stuff. The whole city is sending us supplies. We don't have any people. Don't go in there. Some of the families are in there. They're not going to be able to take this."

He says, "Just keep walking downtown. Just go down. The Con Ed guys, those underground guys, they got nothing. Just go down there. Go."

We turn to leave to go farther down. It is as if the city has been de-defined, blurry gray, can't read the street signs, ash recasting every building in fuzzy out-lines. A catacomb of streets, an unfamiliar maze like a surreal de Chirico or Dalí painting. Time melts.

The farther down we get, the more intense the smells, the more intense the noise. Dawn is coming like we're in a demented snow globe. We start to see actual impact results. The parked cars were flattened, cratered.

We round the next corner, I look over my right shoulder, and two blocks north, there's the press barricade, a line of reporters and satellite trucks. Holy shit, we must be on Church Street. And I look over my left shoulder, and there's the building. What's left of it. There's the facade. You know that twisted facade of the World Trade Center, that image that we all saw on the cover of *Time* magazine.

And just at that moment, at five o'clock in the morning, the sun comes up through the buildings, like Manhattanhenge, and lights up the facade like a house of fire, all red and gold. The sun probably never came through there before. And from the back, this gold, glowing structure twisted and contorted, and somehow still standing, smoke is pouring and swirling in this deep, red sun.

I think—You are here. You are here, like all of those people, eyewitness to the lip edge of the great story. I'm going to pass out. My body is dotting away and becoming an outline, then I am here, then I go black, then here again, then a cutout silhouette and there's the gold gold sun, it's coming up and I'm about to fall away again, and I am standing there in front of the thing that everybody else is watching on TV. We're here, in

the shot, atomizing and reconstituting and atomizing
and reconstituting over and over again. And all of a
sudden I stare at it and it disappears into a black hole,
I am staring and falling down the long corridor of
history and I am standing at the gates of Auschwitz, or
at the edge of Dresden during the firebombing, on the
melting streetcar at Nagasaki, and then further back
I see the pilgrims landing at Plymouth Rock and the
bodies of Native Americans rotting on mats, piles of
skulls, and further back and further back. And the air
turns pixelated like you're changing the channel. And
Connie Hall rips off her mask, heaving with sobs, and
she says, "Why is it so beautiful?"

We realize the whole press corps barricaded up there
is looking at us against the backdrop of the building.
We have no choice. We push the barricade aside, enter-
ing the press area, like the four pizza delivery kids of
the apocalypse. Everyone is staring at us.

First in line is a thirtysomething young woman, wearing a red pantsuit, standing there with a microphone in
her hand, with a huge camera crew behind her.

"What're you guys doing?"

I say, "Well, we're the Church of Pompeii; we're
delivering pizza and food to the first responders."

She says, "Do you want to be on *GMA*?"

I look at Aaron. His face is completely covered in
black dust, and he's got streaking black from tears
under his glasses, and he just looks at me, and I look at
her and say,

"What's *GMA*?"

"Uh. *Good Morning America*."

And Aaron just goes:

(Gestures no, shaking his hands vigorously.)

And as we continued up Sixth Avenue, I had that terrible, sinking feeling of regret.

I realized we made a huge mistake.

Your destiny, your innermost, deepest convictions, these are the things that make you who you are. Your truth, your justice, your guts, your voice; the moment the spotlight comes to you, you use it. You speak out and you speak your truth; that's what everything in my life told me to do. You speak out. And I blew it. I fucked up. I held back.

Justice is a shared notion. When it comes to you, you speak it, on behalf of everyone. That story that we're all being told, all the time, that we share together—our truth needs to be shared. And spoken clearly.

Silence is as good as a lie. And there is no greater lie then the one you use to kill people. We could all tell the killing was just starting.

I'd never been asked to be on television before. I said to myself, "If I ever get those five minutes back, I'm going to say, 'We're New Yorkers. We're picking up the pieces. We're wading through ash; we're stepping over bodies. We're delivering pizza and coffee. And we don't want you to start a war. We don't want you to kill innocents in our names.'"

And I could tell that that's not what's going to be said on TV.

And sure enough, with the clouds of acrid smoke swirling all around, the war chants grew, and the jingoistic revenge machine revved into high gear.

Protests against the wars, Afghanistan and Iraq, around the world became a full-time occupation, you remember this?

Because it wasn't true. Everybody knew it.

Colin Powell at the United Nations with low-grade Nigerian uranium, George Bush talking about WMDs and Saddam—we knew there was no connection to 9/11, it was like a bad play, bad actors.

But we couldn't stop it. The Truth had failed.

And we sat and watched in silence, nothing we could do. We knew that hundreds of thousands of people were on their way to being killed, for no reason.

And looking down, a sense of total powerlessness watching CNN, bomb's-eye view. The cameras on the tips of the Tomahawk missiles coming down off the planes. A person looks very much like an ant. Until the moment the camera cuts, and that person is vaporized.

We had been manipulated in our most vulnerable moment. We had been told to climb, to climb, to climb.

You could find the truth, the reality of it, if you wanted to. On the covers of foreign newspapers not censored by the US media. Children, decapitated by bombs. Pictures of heads on the sand. A child with no arms—none, bloody stumps—shrieking in terror.

The cancer rate in the city of Basra, due to depleted uranium flying around the streets from our tank shells, went to 40 percent among children.

Whole families blown to smithereens. Children doused in their parents' blood, shot at checkpoints, shrieking in horror.

And friends coming home with missing limbs, or missing synapses, or not coming home at all. Civilians dying. Hundreds of thousands of them dying. Horrors unspeakable that were not being reported in the press.

I thought of the war as a kind of deep trauma, almost like American DNA—that we couldn't see, but evident in every moment.

We have those historical imprints.

I know the intergenerational trauma of the Holocaust, it runs in my veins; that's the way it works. Your DNA has an imprint.

I thought of my two grandfathers. One, a Yiddish poet who left his village in Poland at seven at night, story goes, because he heard the Nazis were coming the next morning. The moment they heard he said, "Pack your bags. Now. We're getting out. Right now." And fled all the way, for five long years, to Kazakhstan, where my father was born two weeks before the end of the war. And all of his relatives, and all my grandmother's brothers and sisters, nine brothers and sisters, who stayed until seven the next morning, who didn't leave immediately, who spent the night and said, "We're going to leave tomorrow," they all went to the gas chambers.

That grandfather, hypervigilant, always pointing to something on the horizon in my mind. "See it coming; see the Iraq War coming; see the brutality coming; see what's on the horizon to come to kill us, and get out. Get out. Doesn't matter who else gets out—you're getting out."

That hypervigilance always with me. But my other grandfather, the Italian tailor, arrived in America, couldn't speak English, committed suicide in 1946 when my mother was five years old. He drank a gallon of wine, my aunt Millie told me, and hanged himself. A sad man in a strange place, never found his footing. An Italian with no family. He had enough of life. And he had enough rope—that one also always with me.

One grandfather saying, "You're going to survive everything, no matter what is coming at you." The other one saying, "Fuck it. I'm getting drunk. And I'm out." The visionary versus oblivion. Faith versus mortality.

Like a murmur that's in your ear, that's an outline, that's sitting just behind you, trying to warn you of something that's coming.

The oil under that desert that we went to get, that was the truth.

The truth was we blew them up because of oil.

Oil. The earth's great buried trauma.

Oil is the DNA of evolution. The oil is the DNA of the last mass extinction. It's literally the animals. Extract the DNA of the last mass extinction to bring about the current one.

And so it came for us. Not just in Iraq. Here, we were going to be pulled in its trammel.

Down in the earth's bones was some deep scar to be summoned and extracted. And we were going to fracture those bones. Split apart and get at marrow inside.

I saw it coming. I saw the oil coming for us. And when I saw it, it led me to Texas.

IT'S A DAMN SHAME

"It's a damn shame," says Garland. "You see this rash?" He lifts up his arm; he's got a horrible, scaly red rash all over his arms. "H2S gas, chronic exposure, that's what it will do to you. And Flo can hardly breathe. We can only be here for an hour or so before we start to feel really ill, so we're gonna give you your toxic tour as quick as we can."

May 2008. I'm in a place called Booger County, Texas.

That whole county had been overrun by something that nobody had ever heard of, called *fracking*.

Image of flaring gas wells.

Garland Sugar and his wife, Florence—call her Flo—the Sugars from Booger—had built their dream house.

Every room was done up in wood, you know, wainscoting, from different Texas woods. There was horse show memorabilia, and saddles, and ranchers' whips and ropes. There were spurs that had been refashioned into coasters. And if you looked up at the ceiling, mirroring wood inlay in the floor, the Lone Star.

And a small structure outside, without which no Texas ranch is complete, a smokehouse. For making their own sweet and savory beef jerky.

I'd never met anyone who was more proud of their house . . . or more disgusted that they couldn't live in it.

They were getting rashes and hives and heart palpitations and dizzy spells, because all around them were gas fields and flare stacks. Every little corner of this entire county, fracking wells, spewing out methane and hydrogen sulfide.

As we go past several frack gas wells, down a country dirt road, Garland says, "Roll the window down. Don't breathe too much of this now, because you're gonna get sick." I said, "Wow. That smells like 9/11." That's when he put his hand on my shoulder and we both cried.

How the hell did I get here?

Image of the lush forest of Pennsylvania.

The oil and the gas had come for all of us. And it came for me too.

In 2008, the United States was in the middle of the largest natural gas and oil drilling and fracking campaign in history. And they knocked on my door too, in the upper Delaware River basin in Pennsylvania, the place of my family's first home. Built by hand by my mother and father. A mile from the river, in the watershed for sixteen million people, including NYC and Philadelphia. The beautiful wetlands I grew up on, ponds and pine forests and clean, clean water everywhere. And thousands and thousands of trout streams. Some of the most beautiful, pristine woods on earth. I don't know how many of you are acquainted with streams. I grew up running up and down the stream with my brothers, over and over again. And it seemed to be the source of all life. Because it is. You need water for life.

The gas drillers offered us $4,750 an acre to drill on nearly twenty acres—that was nearly $100,000—to do the F-word, it's just like it sounds. Fracking for natural gas. They said, "Look, just take it; it's free money. You'll hardly ever notice us. We might not even drill. It's just like a fire hydrant in the middle of your field."

But then some neighbors of mine did research—here's what the frackers were injecting into the ground: two to seven million gallons of water infused with seven hundred chemicals, many of them carcinogens and neurotoxins.

And most everybody in my county lived off a water well that was coming directly out of the ground.

In fact, one million people in the state of Pennsylvania depend on groundwater. The mother needs to be pure.

"There's no problem here. We don't use any chemicals," said the gas industry. And my father said, "Josh, a hundred thousand dollars is nothing to sneeze at."

Well, I said, "Look, I don't know who to believe; I don't know what the truth is here." Is it my neighbors who are talking about chemicals and groundwater that's ruined? Or is it the gas industry that's saying we're going to pay you a lot of money and this is environmentally friendly? Who to believe? Who is telling the truth?

They were fracking just fifty miles away in Dimock, Pennsylvania. So I went. And I brought a camera.

First interview, Norma Fiorentino, the trailer on
the corner, her water well had exploded on New Year's
Day. Everybody was off at church, and she came home,
and the concrete casing was blown all over the yard.
Then people started to trade stories—people's laundry
machines were running water that had turned black.
Their animals were dying. Their kids were getting sick.
Then at once several families discovered they could
light their water on fire right out of the tap, just a few
months after drilling.

I was hooked.

Was I actually going to become a kind of natural
gas drilling detective? I was pulling at the threads of a
mystery.

I heard reports of people who could light their water
on fire right near fracking in Colorado.

Horrific images of fracking and ruined water.

I got in my beat-up '92 Camry, and on a $2,500
budget from a few donations, I shot thirty out of
thirty-one days all across the country. One story led to
another, one state to the next. Pennsylvania, Colorado,
Wyoming, Texas, New Mexico, Arkansas. I discovered
an environmental catastrophe like nothing I'd ever
seen before. The whole country was getting fracked.
And everywhere the industry went, water was ruined;
the air was poisoned; the land had been scarred, ripped
apart, and toxified. Halliburton trucks and toxic pits

and machinery spewing black smoke everywhere in residential neighborhoods.

There was a health crisis. People had peripheral neuropathy, skin rashes, cancers, brain damage, ear damage. They had strange illnesses from breathing in volatile organic compounds and BTEX chemicals—endocrine disrupters that would harm adults, children, and even embryonic development in vitro. People had lost their sense of smell; they had lost their sense of taste. Weird, phantom illnesses. Workers on the gas rigs were dying of mysterious cancers or experiencing paralysis in their limbs. And nobody was reporting on this. Nobody.

I slept on the side of the road, or on people's couches, or at rest stops. I had the entire, what I thought was a film, in this one little bag full of two hundred tapes. No copies. I would go to the bathroom with it when I stopped at a truck stop. I wouldn't let it out of my sight for a second. I slept with it under my pillow. I was holding the people's truth in that bag. And the truth had to get out.

HOW DO THINGS CHANGE?

It was like the template of America
that existed in people's minds was not
matching up with reality. There was
a vibration. It was like America had
evaporated into a hologram or a mirage,
left them in a new landscape, immigrants
to an unjust land.

For many people it was an introduction to the basic idea of political hypocrisy. It was as if there were two Americas—one for the oil companies and another for everyone else. ExxonMobil, Halliburton, Chevron—American companies whose MO was always to have a different standard for how they treated white Americans from how they treated people of color in the developing world, now bringing their hypocrisy home and recklessly destroying the lives of white people here just like they did people of color everywhere.

And Rex Tillerson, that doughy, dimpled denier, CEO of ExxonMobil, the number-one fracking company in the world, actually sued to keep fracking out of his own community in Texas.

But another strand of American DNA woke up at that moment. The rebellious gene. People were changing because of this. People who had never gotten involved politically, when the oil and gas industry came and invaded their lives, they changed.

Like Susan Frye in Guy, Arkansas, which had an earthquake swarm of a thousand fracking-induced earthquakes in six months. She was obsessed with the frack-quakes. She had a plumb bob that was tied to the bottom of her coffee table. She would stare at it. And every time that plumb bob moved, she would run to the United States Geological Survey site and say, "Sure enough, there was another quake." Most of these were microquakes. But then a 4.7 came, and put cracks in the walls of the local high school. And knocked the earthquake lady's husband out of his La-Z-Boy chair. And I imagine, as he hit the ground, something changed.

Or Amy Elsworth in Colorado. Her water was so flammable that it would produce explosions in her bathroom sink. She was showering in the dark, because she was afraid the spark from her light bulb would ignite and blow her across the street in the middle of the shower. And I can imagine her standing there, fumbling in the dark, naked, looking for a towel, dripping wet. Something changed.

Or the Gee family, five generations on the same land in Pennsylvania. Shell built a six-well, horizontal frack pad about 150 feet from Jeremiah Gee's mother's bedroom window. Where all those volatile organic compounds could waft down the hill, right into her bedroom. They had to sell their house to Shell. And sign a nondisclosure agreement stating that they would never speak about this. They traded their First Amendment rights just to get out of gasland. And I imagine, as they closed the door for the last time, and realized they didn't need to lock it, something changed.

Or Terry Greenwood. Died of glioblastoma. Brain cancer. A farmer in Western Pennsylvania. Nine out of ten calves, just after the fracking had taken place on his farm, were stillborn. The last one that came out dead was blind, with pure white eyes. He was tucking the calf in a plastic bag, into a meat freezer, when he said, "I'm going to find out why my cows died. They were drinking out of that pond water that they were dumping the fracking well into. I know that's not good." And as his wife walked away from his grave site realizing that she buried him before the stillborn calf, something changed.

Or Frank Finan, a woodworker from Dimock, Pennsylvania, who always wore his Pink Floyd *Dark Side of the Moon* baseball hat; his wife had died of cancer six months earlier, and with the money that they were setting aside for their retirement, to grow old, he purchased a FLIR camera, a $50,000 camera that could see methane that was invisible to the naked eye. He uncovered—a woodworker with this insane equipment—that the gas wells, and that the fracking wells, were leaking and shooting huge clouds of methane directly into the atmosphere. Methane itself is one hundred times more potent than carbon dioxide in the atmosphere in terms of greenhouse warming. Clouds of invisible methane. A study from Cornell estimated that fracked gas was, in fact, worse than coal in terms of global warming impacts; that if we develop fracked gas on a large scale, we could accelerate warming well beyond our control and frack ourselves to a global warming apocalypse. And when Frank saw that, something changed.

And then I saw the map of the future: three hundred proposed fracked-gas power plants.

Huge, thousand-megawatt power plants, strewn all across the United States—the Obama administration was pushing this as the next wave of energy and electricity generation. This would require two million new fracking wells, and hundreds of thousands of miles of pipelines. A horrific vision of what was to come in the next decade of energy development for the United States.

All this misery and danger instead of simply developing renewable energy, WHICH WE KNOW CAN POWER EVERYTHING IN THE UNITED STATES.

I saw there simply was nothing bigger than this in terms of energy, environment, politics, justice. Fracking had to be stopped. And the truth about it had to be told—no matter what the consequences.

That's when I realized *I had changed.*

This was going to be a fight, and I knew it. But I was going to be loyal to my grandfather. He delivered my blood from the gas chambers, I was not about to let the promised land become gasland.

GASLAND was carried on the backs of people hosting community screenings; the film was passed from person to person, state to state, continent to continent. Went on HBO and then on TV in thirty-two countries with an estimated audience of about fifty million on five continents. Across the world we began organizing. The truth was on the march.

I had no idea, however, what was about to come after us.

SCENE 5

POISONING
THE WELL

Josh reaches for his glass of water.
When he's about to drink, a black
glob of something disgusting, like oil
or chemicals, falls from above into his
glass, staining the water. He looks at it
in disgust.

First, in the middle of the night, an email from the *New York Times*, informing me that a twenty-one-point, ten-page hit-sheet called "Debunking *GASLAND*" had been put out by the oil industry. It claimed that the flammable water scene was a fake—and they attacked virtually every scene and claim in the film.

We scrambled to get together our proof—all of our water tests and scientific testimony—and sent that to every reporter we could find.

Josh pours a second glass of water. Again, just as he puts it to his lips a disgusting black glob drops into it, contaminating it. He stares at the second glass.

I went on *The Daily Show*. Jon Stewart came back to me in the dressing room before we went on, and he said, "You know we got five hundred faxes this morning from someplace called Energy In Depth." And I said, "Well, that's the gas industry." "So, yeah, yeah, yeah, we know; we're not falling for that." But he still asked me the question on the air. He still asked me, "What about these critics?"

But more and more attacks come in the press.

And now I am noticing that at all the *GASLAND* screenings for communities, hostile questions from industry plants attack my credibility. Negative op-eds

come out in right-wing publications about how
GASLAND is a "fake documentary."

*Josh pours a third glass of water. Again, just
as he puts his lips to the glass a disgusting
black glob falls into it, contaminating it.
He stares at the third glass.*

And it becomes clear to me that this is having
an impact on the very people I am trying to get to.
I wanted to bring the stories of average Americans
directly to the people affected—to the folks in
gas-drilling territory. But the message is being
contaminated.

Pretty soon screenings around the country get
downright hostile. There is a seething, percolating rage
that has been drummed up. You know that rage—Tea
Party, white, down and out, out of work and heavily
armed, mildly or overtly racist, proud of ignorance,
Confederate flag waving, that rage. Not exactly my
best friends. The propaganda is fueling a fire—I am
now no longer Pennsylvania's favorite son, but the
bespectacled New York Jew-liberal who is tearing up
their lottery ticket. For the first time ever, I am given
the label "Hollywood director."

I'm beginning to be obsessed—constantly checking
the articles being written. Constantly looking over my
shoulder.

Then I find something odd.

In Pennsylvania, I find that when I google "Josh Fox," or the name of the movie, "*GASLAND*," I get what is called a "sponsored link" at the top—a little box, slightly gray but mostly looking like the regular results—that says "The Truth About *GASLAND*." And if you click on it that directs you to a YouTube video, about four minutes long, with a very official but warm-sounding woman explaining calmly why everything in *GASLAND* is fake and thoroughly discredited.

That video shot up to four hundred thousand views. Soon, I found out my name was worth forty cents a click.

And, if you searched in Pennsylvania, then underneath the sponsored link, for several pages of Google results you would get all the conservative and attack websites. Breitbart.com, the *Washington Free Beacon*, Energy In Depth, *HotAir*, TheBlaze—all of these right-wing sites attacking the film.

But, astonishingly, when I got down to New York City and I googled my name, I wouldn't get the ad or the attack sites. I'd get our *New York Times* review, our *Washington Post* rave, and our website. But then, back up to Central Pennsylvania or somewhere that was being fracked? Google my name and boom! "The Truth About *GASLAND*." *Washington Free Beacon*. Energy In Depth. Breitbart.com.

I thought, "That's weird. I thought Google just gave you results."

A glob of black gunk hits Josh's face. Projections appear on Josh's face and desk indicating thousands of drops during this section.

That was just the beginning.

Next, Tom Ridge, former governor of Pennsylvania and the former and first head of the Department of Homeland Security, appointed right after 9/11, signs on to be the chief spokesman for the Marcellus Shale Coalition, a gas industry group that fights environmental regulation of gas drilling. The very next month, the Pennsylvania Department of Homeland Security begins issuing briefs that list anti-fracking protest groups as possible "ecoterrorists," claiming that environmental extremism trending toward ecoterrorism and criminality is on the rise in Pennsylvania.

Then it is revealed that Pennsylvania Homeland Security is showing up at fracking protests, spying on gas-drilling activists and *GASLAND* screenings, but they weren't only sending the information to law enforcement; they were sending it to the gas industry.

Just after that the local pro-drilling group in my town sends out an email saying—you see, I told you Josh Fox and those anti-frackers were terrorists.

And just after that, one of the sheds on my parents' property is mysteriously burned to the ground while I am on tour. I return to find that the township supervisor, who is pro-fracking, has sent photos of the burned structure to the Pennsylvania Department of Environmental Protection and gotten me written up on a violation of the Clean Streams Law. So now I am a self-arsonist.

Then the head geologist of Pennsylvania, without knowing my family's history, says that *GASLAND* is a piece of propaganda that even Goebbels would be proud of. So now I am a Nazi.

Then conservative and pro-drilling blogs start to say that *GASLAND* was actually funded by Vladimir Putin as a gambit to stop US and European gas from challenging Russia in the European market. And because we had a Venezuelan immigrant intern at one point that we must also be working directly with Hugo Chávez.

So now I am a Communist.

Communist.

Arsonist.

Terrorist.

Nazi.

And still this was just the beginning.

It's a tsunami of smear and misinformation.

I start getting followed home late at night. One natural gas blog encourages people to do "drive-bys" of my house. I am getting death threats and tweet threats and Facebook promises of decapitation and the rape and murder of my family.

Then, Texas Sharon, an anti-fracking blogger, attends an oil and gas conference and sits in on some of their closed-door strategy sessions. She records a gas-drilling PR rep bragging that they have hired psy-ops officers, returned from Iraq, to sow confusion in landowners in Pennsylvania.

Psy-ops—psychological operations—are employed in a war zone to destabilize a population. Psy-ops were used by the American military in Vietnam, in Iraq. And here the gas industry is employing former psy-ops experts to be used against landowners in Texas and in Pennsylvania.

They use terms like "counterinsurgency." "Strategies for managing outrage." "Destabilization of communities."

These are terms of war.

And I was so rattled by this smear campaign, and so knocked off base, that I started to be very nervous all the time, like someone was watching me. I would go to Barbara Arrindell's house, and borrow an AR-15. I'd trained with the military for several of my films. The weapon was comforting. So I would go and clear every room in my house. You know, tear open shower curtains with the AR-15, check every closet. And then sit down with my rifle and drink half a bottle of whiskey, and watch *The Hurt Locker* till 4 a.m.—not a good combo. The first time I ever felt fear in my work, ever, but there it was. Uncomfortable, raw fear.

Josh takes out the whiskey, pours it, stops to look up, then shoots it quickly down the hatch.

Then, a new wrinkle. The gas industry actually started to make movies. You can't really call them documentaries, because they were entirely made up of lies. But they copied our model, sending their films out to grassroots pro-drilling orgs.

Andrew Breitbart at breitbart.com teams up with known ultra-conservative charlatans Phelim McAleer, Ann McElhinney, and even press lothario Fred Davis, and two films come out. *FrackNation* and *Truthland*.

Oh. And there was a third guy working with that operation. A dark shadowy overlord lurking in the rainswept doorway of the propaganda machine. I will get to him later.

When Breitbart got involved this got deeply personal. They sent hate emails specifically designed to threaten me personally—my upbringing, my character. They highlighted my parents' divorce, the fact that my father was Jewish, my glasses, my hairline, my life in the theater.

They learned I had quit smoking years and years before, and found pictures of me smoking online and ran them as TV ads in pro-fracking campaigns in Ohio—saying how can a smoker be an environmentalist?

And they were following me. Not just at home but around the country. They booked shadow tours of my films—we showed *GASLAND* at hundreds of grassroots venues: Grange halls, churches, theaters, community centers. And they would book a venue across the street to show *Truthland* or *FrackNation* so that they could court newspapers and radio stations to cover "both sides" of the issue.

This takes a real toll. When you are being followed—in real life and online—every move you make becomes a tremor. They get inside your head and it is really, really scary. It is like someone is lurking inside of your skull. They have your personal information. They have clearly researched you and know how you tick. They try to get under your skin. It is deeply effective. You move out of fear. You scramble for safety. It was very hard to not think of that third guy, a guy named Steve Bannon, and Andrew Breitbart when I was trying to fall asleep at night, wondering what their next attack might be.

They are harassing me and following me all over the country with cameras. They take interviews with me from Q and A sessions and rearrange the words to make my sentences say things that I did not say.

Slander. Smear. Misinform. Parade.

All in all, David Fenton, our counterattack strategist, said that the oil industry must have spent $50 to $100 million attacking us.

But then the government starts to buy it. Barack Obama begins to spout natural gas industry talking points in his policy speeches.

The industry spends nearly a billion dollars lobbying for fracking at every level of government.

Hillary Clinton, as secretary of state, begins the "Global Shale Gas Initiative" pushing fracking in thirty countries worldwide.

We plead our case at the Council on Environmental Quality in the White House, then White House environmental policy director Heather Zichal leaves the council to take a lucrative board position at Cheniere Energy, the leading fracking export company in the world.

We unearth the gas industry's own reports that show that they knew their wells failed at alarming rates.

Obama appoints John Deutsch, former CIA director, who has $1.4 million in stock in fracking, as chair of the Department of Energy special panel on fracking.

Time after time, the movement leads with science, democracy, reporting, organizing, sacrifice, and fact.

And time after time the fracking industry, media, and government respond with graft, cronyism, smear, dirty tricks, lobbying, misinformation, intimidation, and litigation.

And as I look back on it now, I get dizzy. The pervasiveness of it. From silencing/killing/coercing my neighbors at the grass roots all the way to lobbying and lying to the president. Media, Government, Industry. Collusion? Conspiracy? Or just straight up how power works? All of our efforts, focused on one story, one truth, to try to flip it. WE won the argument, but we lost the government.

The well was poisoned. The truth at the bottom of a murky toxic puncture.

Rattled and exhausted, we head down to New Orleans to cover the BP oil spill.

WHAT ELSE CAN THEY COVER UP?

It was the first day off in a long time. July 4, 2010. We decided that with our first day off we were going to fly down to New Orleans. We had booked an eco-flight, from Lighthawk, a small plane donated by rich people so that poor documentary filmmakers can lean out the rich person's plane and film eco-catastrophes below.

But the fear is still clinging to me. I've become afraid of things I was never afraid of before. Go home, fear. Answer the phone, fear. Get on a plane, fear.

So I was rattled and shaky, and I didn't want to get on the plane.

But my visionary mind was beckoning, like precognition, it was saying, "You see something there. You're looking down at the gulf." And I saw it—I couldn't explain it. Like a cutout, kindergarten paper doll that kids make—a hallucination—and he was flying, he was falling, falling out of the plane, onto the surface of the gulf. And there he was, like a chalk outline, on the gulf. And I kept seeing it over and over again, falling. What was happening?

Our first stop in Louisiana was to visit Wilma Subra, the MacArthur genius award–winning chemist. She looks like a grandmother who has just baked a nice batch of brownies, kind of like the Oracle in *The Matrix*? And she's got on earrings and a pink sweater, and she comes out to meet us, and she's clearly a genius. She goes, "The volatile organic compounds, the polynuclear aromatic hydrocarbons, are wafting off the surface of the gulf; workers are inhaling this and passing out. And the EPA has approved spreading a dispersant—Corexit, a toxic chemical—onto the toxic oil. And what that is doing is sinking the oil. It's covering it up. It's pushing it down. And the oil is one toxicity, and the Corexit is another toxicity, and combined they are fifteen times the toxicity of either one; and it is spreading the oil all the way through the water column, and sinking it to the ocean floor, where the shrimp breed, and the clams breed, and the oysters breed. And that's where life comes from." And she said, "Generations. The Gulf of Mexico is lost for generations."

And we're driving back—Alex Tyson, my cameraman, and Matt Sanchez, the brilliant cinematographer, I think of him as Little Hands of Concrete . . . Alex answers the phone and he goes, "What?! Holy shit. Really?"

Well, you see, BP and the FAA had been working together. No flights were allowed below three thousand feet. You couldn't get clearance to fly below three thousand feet. I don't know what happens below three thousand feet—if you turn into a pumpkin, or they scramble F-14s, who knows—but no flights are being allowed under three thousand feet.

The *New Orleans Times-Picayune* reported that when reporters were calling the FAA to clear their flights, BP would answer the phone. But nevertheless, Alex is in the backseat going, "Holy shit." Lighthawk tells us we've gotten the first clearance to fly at any altitude we want.

In this life you either run toward your fear or it is forced upon you. There was no way out. I got on the plane.

This plane is the size of a Toyota, two people in the front, one in the third seat, and another one in the back, just this small. And Matt is leaning out the window, and the wind is pushing him back, and he's looking at me: "God, I've never felt wind like that." I've never been on a plane you could open the windows of before.

We get way, way out, fifty miles off the Outer Continental Shelf. There are only twelve rigs like the *Deepwater Horizon*. There were only twelve of them. They were so deep, you had to go five thousand feet to the bottom of the ocean, and then twenty thousand feet below that. That's five miles down. The oil was what they called "abiogenic oil." It wasn't fossil. They didn't know where it came from, or how to control it. And it was bubbling out—millions and millions of barrels.

And then we get there. All of a sudden we are swooping through clouds of gray-black smoke. The relief well is being drilled, and natural gas is coming up off that well and they are flaring it off. There's a hundred-foot ball of flame shooting out of this relief well. And we're swooping through the clouds of smoke; we're swooping through the clouds of this fireball. And then we see it.

First, like brown patches on the surface, and then out a little bit farther—the oil stretched from horizon to horizon, as far as you could see. Like tendrils, like ghosts on the surface, streaking, like when you drop gasoline into a puddle, but the whole ocean. We hadn't seen that on the news.

And I said to the pilot, "Roger, get us up to three thousand feet, just so I can see what it looks like." And he goes up to three thousand feet. And you look down,

and it just looks like a summer's day. Sunlight rippling
on the surface of the ocean. Can't see it. Not there.
Gone. The oil magically vanishes like a mirage. And I
said, "Bring us back down; bring us back down; let's
see how far this goes." And we go down. And there it
is. It goes on for miles, and miles, and miles, as far as
we could see, ten miles in every direction.

Oil.

And that's when the vision came true.

Something inside me fractured at that moment.
Split off and fell out of the plane. And floated down.
Onto the surface. I don't know, a piece of me? A mirror
self, like a falling shadow coming to meet itself on
the surface. Falling and falling, it landed there like an
outline, like in a murder scene. It went down, deep,
under. And I felt it go. Lost and drowned.

And the ocean looked very sick, and angry, like it
was about to boil.

It was seventy-five days into the spill and we hadn't
seen any pictures like this on the news. Yes—we saw
oiled pelicans and tar balls on beaches, but nothing
of this scale and scope. Clearly there was collusion
between the oil industry, the government, and the
media.

And I thought to myself, "If they can cover up
the greatest environmental catastrophe that's ever
happened to the United States, what else can they
cover up?"

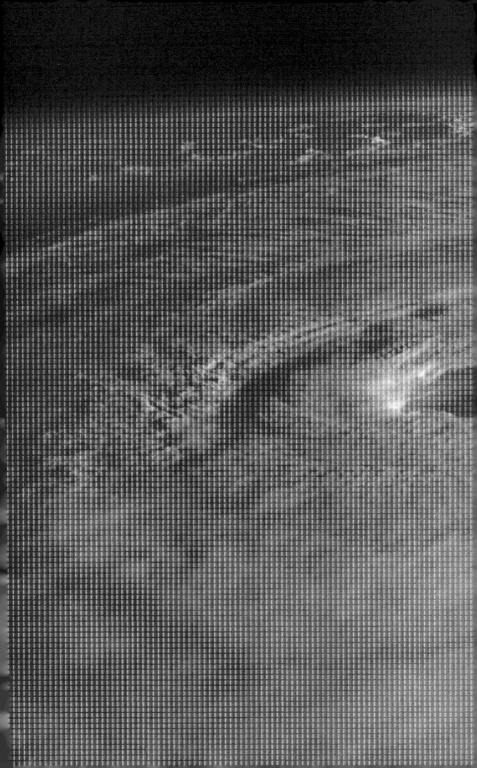

SCENE 7

ALGORITHM OF OCEAN WAVES

I had a dream that night. That I was digging at Ground Zero. Underneath the subway that used to run underneath the Twin Towers. And I found the bones of the terrorists who flew the planes. And I put them in an urn. And I put them up on my shelf. At night, they would sing. And they

would laugh at me. Then I could hear them having sex.
The bones. Have you ever been trapped in a room where
other people are having sex? It's awful. Noises like you're
eating something, and you can't turn around. You really
want to, but you can't turn around. The bones are making these noises, eating or fucking, and I couldn't touch
them. And then I realized, I'm Antigone. And I ran out to
Broadway to bury their remains. They were my brothers
too. And I was swarmed upon by the New York Giants.
And they ripped me apart. And I think they ate me. They
ground up my bones and my brain stem, and fed them to
cows who went mad.

Somewhere on the Atlantic Ocean, a cloud forms
off the top of a crest of a wave. The algorithm of ocean
waves, the mathematics of mist, beginning a counter-
clockwise spin in a way that's never been seen before.
Far, far off the coast. Rising.

An upward spiral.

Water droplets.

Dancing mist.

Water cresting in a different pattern than has ever
been seen on the planet.

A warming ocean spitting up more of itself.

Into the vapor.

The warm air holding the water molecules, gathering
velocity, gathering steam.

I woke up from the dream drenched in sweat.

My bed floating.

A wave building far off on the horizon.

Coming toward us.

Can you see it?

PART TWO

I was doing a theater workshop in Indonesia. With all these dancers and actors from different countries. And the Indonesian dancers told a story about how the Dutch had come to Bali, to see the great Balinese medicine dance. And they'd raised all this money to take the Balinese medicine dancers and bring them to the Netherlands, with all their paraphernalia, and their regalia and their beautiful ritual. And they got all these foundations to put up funds and sold out a huge theater. They brought them to the stage, a sold-out, thousand-seat theater, and the Dutch said, "Okay, here you go. Please do your medicine dance!" And the dancers looked at them and out at the huge audience, and they said, "Well, who's sick?"

SCENE 8

VENUS USED TO HAVE AN OCEAN

"The Earth's temperature has gone up by one degree Celsius," Bill McKibben, the famed writer on climate change, tells me as I interview him.

"One degree. That doesn't sound like so much. But it's enough to get everything on Earth that's supposed to stay frozen to start melting."

He continues, a kind of New-England-ice-cold matter-of-factness in his voice.

"One degree means that we've got a five percent wetter atmosphere. We're evaporating so much more water, because of the heat, and five percent is enough to completely alter the way that water moves around the planet. Water is moving in a way that it never has during human civilization. All that water goes up, it's gotta come down—in downpour, deluge, and flood. Unprecedented extreme storms." In other places, severe drought.

"Five percent wetter since the dawn of industrial times. That's an enormous physical change to the basics of the planet."

Michael Mann, at the University of Pennsylvania a few days later, said, "Well, we have one degree of warming now. We have enough carbon dioxide and methane in the upper atmosphere to bring us to 1.5 degrees no matter what we do." Because there's a radiative effect that will last decades. So we're going to get to 1.5 no matter what.

And now our oceans are absorbing heat, they're warming up, they're killing coral reefs, these amazing, biodiverse, colorful places that are the building blocks of all the biodiversity in the ocean. The Atlantic Ocean hit 87–88 degrees during hurricane season in 2016. Almost body temperature. It's like it's having a bad day, like it's having a fever dream. Churning up the largest storms we have ever seen on the planet.

But it gets worse.

Because at two degrees of warming, which is right around the corner, we bring about an unstoppable process that will melt enough ice on Greenland and Antarctica to bring about five to nine METERS of sea-level rise. Meters. Not feet. That's sixteen and a half to thirty feet.

That means much of New York, Philadelphia, Boston, Providence, Baltimore, half of Bangladesh, many of the cities in the Mediterranean go underwater. That's at twenty-seven feet. The coast of Louisiana gone. New Orleans becomes an island. Half of Florida, underwater. That's sea-level rise. Everything else changes. Forests become deserts. Extreme drought. Extreme flood. Extreme weather becomes something that's just every other day. Ecosystems collapse. Fifty percent of all the species on the planet go extinct. That's a lot of goodbyes.

And I'm reminded of what James Hansen, formerly of NASA, now at Columbia University, said to me.

"Venus used to have an ocean." Now it's seven hundred degrees at the surface of Venus, hot enough to melt lead, because of a runaway greenhouse effect.

Lester Brown, environmental analyst and founder of Worldwatch Institute and Earth Policy Institute, said in 2010 to my camera, "We need an eighty percent reduction in carbon emissions by 2020, to save the Greenland ice sheet." Losing the Greenland ice sheet would represent thirty-nine feet of sea-level rise.

Two degrees is a scorched-earth hell because it's an

average. Africa cooks by four degrees. Everyone who lives on coastlines has to move, the ocean never stays put. The United Nations estimates, because of droughts, fire, sea-level rise, lack of food, and basic destabilization, that there will be a billion climate refugees swarming to find new homes on this planet when we reach two degrees Celsius. A billion displaced people.

Lester Brown continues—we talk a lot about failed states. Afghanistan. Somalia. Places that have no functional government anymore. No one is in charge, no police force; there's no fire department; failed states.

Lester Brown says at two degrees, we're looking at a failed civilization. What does that look like?

Just ask the people in San Juan. The whole thing collapses.

And all of these climate scientists and reporters—smeared and maligned, as I had been, by the oil industry. And Rex Tillerson, that doughy, dimpled denier, CEO of ExxonMobil, famously suggested that we would adapt to climate change by moving our crop production areas. Simply move Iowa up to Canada, that kind of thing. It is almost as if they say absurd things to distract us or something.

Climb. Climb. Climb.

We get to two degrees in 2030.

And the *Guardian* is now reporting that the average of all climate estimates says that we're on a path to a scorching three degrees.

A billion people homeless. Wars break out. Everything

falls apart. A vision of the apocalypse that we're careening toward at ever-quickening rates.

What do we do with the vision of the apocalypse, the scientific certainty of a *Mad Max* future?

The temptation with a truth of this magnitude is simply to put it in a box, a Pandora's box, and put it away and not open it till later. Don't open it till doomsday.

Or, in America, don't open it until the election.

And something remarkable happened in the last election. Someone started actually telling the truth about fracking, climate, economics. Bernie Sanders. With stark honesty he was telling us of unfair economics and tyrannical oligarchs and corporations run amok, an unvarnished reality in his confrontational Brooklyn twang. This was a truth that a lot of Americans, myself included, needed to hear.

And luckily, he asked me to advise his campaign on fracking and support him, and I did. And after a few months on the campaign trail, speaking alongside Bernie and witnessing the cheering throngs of tens of thousands at rallies, and the unmistakable feeling that something unprecedented, something revolutionary was happening, he appointed me to the Democratic Platform Committee to go and help write the democratic platform, that next great chapter, that aspirational document of what we were going to become as a nation.

SCENE 9

DEMOCRATLAND

And my great friend, Nomiki Konst,
the spitfire Greek American, devil in
my ear, thorn in the Democratic Party
consciousness, reporter from TYT, was
also appointed. She was hyped. "We've
gotta change the party! The Democrats
have lost a thousand seats in the last

eight years! They're clueless!" And at 8 a.m. the next morning Amtrak pulls in. The revolution comes to Orlando.

Home of Disney World, you know, Tomorrowland, Frontierland, Adventureland, Fantasyland, now Democratland.

A long roller-coaster ride through all the issues laid out in front of us, the American people. We are going to write the aspirational document called "The Democratic Platform." Down to Florida to fight for the soul of the Democratic Party, a queasy loop-de-loop log flume with singing puppets, lobbyists, activists, fund-raising bundlers, horse traders, and heroes.

Now the platform is not usually something that's contentious or eventful in any way. It's usually, "Ra ra ra, let's get behind the candidate." You know—Michael Dukakis, Bill Clinton, Barack Obama, the nominee, the campaign, they generally write the platform. But since there was no nominee, and since Hillary Clinton and Bernie Sanders had very different philosophies, this platform hearing was actually going to be a firestorm.

We were going to vote on over two hundred different amendments. What was the party actually going to be? What were our principles?

Were we going to be the party of FDR, of the New Deal, of the Great Society, of public trust and public responsibility? Or were we going to be the party of triangulation and neoliberalism that was created by Bill and

Hillary Clinton and Obama? Yes, liberal on social and identity issues, but conservative on everything else. You remember Bill Clinton, the Bill Clinton of Wall Street deregulation, of NAFTA, the crime bill—many of us called them the "Republicrats."

So this was going to be a fight in Orlando. Bernie appointed his best, a team that really could've been called the "Aspirers." Bill McKibben, the great climate change activist; Nina Turner, the ferocious state senator from Ohio; Ben Jealous, former head of the NAACP; Dr. Cornel West, the great civil rights activist; Native American leader Deborah Parker; and many, many more. Fabulous speakers, enormous integrity.

Now, I was to play a bit part. I was to propose two amendments. One for a total ban on fracking—that was coming from the Bernie campaign. The other, that I'd written myself, a ban on fracked-gas power plants. That terrifying new map of three hundred proposed fracked-gas power plants, we as Democrats, how could we support that? My personal mission was to change that course. We were not going to let the planet Earth go down that path, that path of three degrees' warming, that accelerated climate change path, that path to two million new fracking wells, that's where we were going to draw the line in the sand.

Unfortunately, we knew that the Clinton campaign supported fracked gas. As I said, Secretary Clinton had promoted the Global Shale Gas Initiative, selling fracking in thirty-two countries strategically. To

Hillary, fracking was going to be a hedge against the Russians in Europe. Fracking was going to be a hedge against OPEC in Africa. Fracking was going to be a US export to China and Asia and Japan, and revitalize the American economy. Forget American water supply; forget the climate. This is geopolitics. You get fracked; you get fracked; you get fracked; everybody gets fracked.

The setting for this ideological grudge match is the dingiest Ramada-Tree-Double-Omni-Wyndham-Suite-Hampton-Inn that Orlando can muster. Maybe Debbie Wasserman Schultz's relatives owned it—I don't know. But it had beige walls, beige carpeting, beige tables, beige dust, and beige food. Our mission: to not let the Democratic platform policy become equally beige.

The Clinton delegates outnumbered the Bernie delegates by about 55 percent to 45 percent, so unless we had real magic, we were going to lose on every vote.

So *woosh!* around the first corner. Tilt-a-Whirl into the first plenary. Immediately, I see we have a culture clash on our hands. The Clinton folks are showing up with their red, white, and blue Styrofoam hats, their three-piece suits, their cuff links. They're looking at the whip in the corner. The whip is telling them exactly how they're supposed to vote. This is the establishment and they are going to vote in line.

Then the Bernie delegation streams in, with red, white, and blue hair—activists, you know, young people, political groups finally getting a chance to duke it out with the establishment, activist T-shirts, buttons and signs, sort of like a cross between a CBGB hardcore matinee and the Model United Nations conference at your local high school.

You know, you'll never believe how much politics is like your local high school.

And now we're ramping it up; it's a steep climb—the first amendment to go is the raise of Social Security premiums. People are coming in to testify; valiant folks come in to say that their grandparents can't pay for their medicine and food at the same time with these premiums. So senior citizens on Social Security are eating cat food just so they can afford their medicine.

Whoosh! Fly through the whip on the Clinton side. Thumbs down. They vote down Social Security raise. Clinton delegates are looking at us, saying, "Oh my God, I can't believe I just voted against that." Nomiki Konst—my colleague, the spitfire of TYT, Greek-American gadfly—stands up, and she furiously pounds her fist on the table and says, "Are you Democrats?!," prompting Congresswoman Maxine Waters, sitting directly behind her, to start shushing her.

It's getting late, and Donna Brazile is walking the room, asking who wants a Jägermeister shot. She's hit the bar early, she's passing out drinks from a tray— "Who wants a Jägerbomb?"

Then *aaaaaaaahh!* all the way down into the pit of genocide in Gaza. Dr. Cornel West gives the most passionate speech of the night: "The condition of truth is always to allow suffering to speak! The great rabbi Abraham Joshua Heschel said that 'indifference to evil is more evil than evil itself.' In Gaza, two thousand killed, five hundred babies killed. What is going on in this country? Are we so debilitated by either the money flowing or indifference in our hearts? I would hope not. That's what the legacy of Martin Luther King and Dorothy Day and so many others was all about. . . . If we are not able to deal with that, then we're in the same condition this party was in eighty years ago when it didn't want to deal with Jim Crow, didn't want to deal with lynching, locked in a state of denial."

Clinton whip votes it down. They vote it down. My stomach is in my throat. My heart is pounding. We're in free fall. Rancor and dissent are everywhere. John Lewis, the great civil rights hero, is trying to gavel us to order.

And up we climb, and then all of a sudden . . . the ratchet stops . . . Something has happened! The mighty and righteous Nina Turner announces she's made contact with the union leader on the Clinton side, and they've come to an agreement on minimum wage. Fifteen dollars an hour—a living wage—will be the Democratic Party position!

It's a beautiful moment. The whole Sanders delegation stands; the whole Clinton delegation stands. Ten people make speeches, five from each side, led by Nina Turner. It's actually what we are looking for: unity. The fight for $15, the movement that was started

in Chicago, has won, the fast-food workers taking
to the streets have won. It is now the policy of the
Democratic Party. Fifteen dollars. We are Democrats
again. We are fighting against Donald Trump, and we
want to win. We're going to reconcile, and we're going
to heal. We're going to WIN!

Clap the gavel. It's 1 a.m.

We're done for today. Nomi and I run for the bar to
discuss the revolution, and it is closed. Donna Brazile
knew something. Should have had a Jägerbomb.

The next morning, we're up early. It's going to be
a long day. Down the log flume of Flint, Michigan;
the mad teacup ride of marijuana legalization—which
passes, by one vote, when the Clinton whip accidentally
goes to the bathroom! And rowing in the rancid tides of
"It's a Small World" for immigration reform.

It's getting late in the day . . . the last day. And I
know I'm not off the hook yet. The fracking amendments are coming up. I get a tap on the shoulder.
"Josh, come back here."

It's the "negotiator" (he or she shall remain name-
less) summoning me to the back room. Yes, there is a
back room, and yes, so much of what really goes on in
politics goes on back there. I feel special, but also a bit
worried. What's up?

The negotiator says to me, "I just got off the phone
with Bernie. He's willing to take the fight for the fracking ban all the way to the convention in Philadelphia."
The floor almost fell away from me. I was shocked and

honored. I didn't know Bernie was so deeply committed to the fracking ban. It moved me profoundly that Bernie was willing to fight for our anti-fracking movement at the Democratic Convention in two weeks, like someone out there had actually been listening to us for all these years. I was ready to roll up my sleeves and go out and brawl right there.

Then Bill McKibben walks in the room—from Vermont, very close to Bernie Sanders, lanky, Sunday-school-teacher, staid, stoic New Englander wearing a Boston Red Sox hat. I'm wearing my Yankees hat, the emotional Italian Jew. As always, we're an unlikely alliance.

I turn to Bill. He says, wisely, that the real fight is always in our activism, and our movement. And this time probably after Hillary is elected. He said, "I'm not sure having that kind of confrontation at the convention is productive. But these are your amendments. It's up to you. What do you want to do?"

This was a pickle. We knew Bernie was not going to be the nominee. Would I throw the Democrats into a huge floor fight on national TV? We'd been fighting for this fracking ban for ten years with everything we had. My stomach was in knots.

I knew that to acquiesce to Hillary and walk away from the fracking ban would completely destroy my credibility, and enrage the movement—rightly so. Seventeen million Americans lived within one mile of a fracking well. Fracking victims throughout the nation

were enraged and furious at Hillary. We had to be true
to our principles, to ourselves, somehow.

I said, "Give me ten minutes." Then I called all the
fracking leaders from around the country, in Wyoming,
Texas, and New York. I said, "We have a choice. We can
burn it down over the fracking ban on the Democratic
platform in Philadelphia." I said, "But it could do us
real damage if we're out there fighting with each other."
I said, "I wrote another amendment to ban the three
hundred fracked-gas power plants. I actually think it's
more important. What if we posit that as the compromise? What do you think?" Tony Ingraffea from Cornell
pipes up. He says, "I can write a plan to phase out
fracked shale gas completely in five to eight years. Let's
deliver that plan to the Clinton campaign, as our terms
for getting out the anti-fracking vote." I love this; I said,
"We'll get the door open, we'll stop the power plants,
we'll unify the party, and we'll kill fracking for good in
the United States." Every person said, "Yes, that's a great
strategy. Let's do it." No fucking way we're going to help
Donald Trump in Philly. No way.

So Bill McKibben and I, and Jane Kleeb from Bold,
Nebraska, and many others, collaborated on this new
unity amendment. We would incentivize renewable
energy, which we know can power everything in the
United States (and the world)—solar and wind—over
the fracked-gas power plants.

Renewable energy would rise! And frontline
communities, people of color and Native Americans,

would be at the table when energy decisions were being made.

We wrote it out and sent it to the Clinton back room. In the gallery outside, in the audience portion, hundreds of fractivists were angrily screaming and cheering for a fracking ban, knowing that these amendments were coming up.

And the amendment comes back. The Clinton campaign says the language is okay. No fracked-gas power plants. Renewable energy. I break down in tears in the hallway. Bill McKibben is like, "Oh, emotion man, with the crying and the—" And I'm like, "Bill, I'm happy."

So we get out, announce the unity amendment. The whole Clinton side stands. The whole Sanders side stands. Dr. West gives me a fist bump that turns into a GIF on Facebook. We've brought the party together. It's an incredible moment of victory.

When we announce what we've done, the angry anti-fracking mob in the back of the room, two hundred people, instead of screaming, they start cheering. They're applauding; they're pumping their fists in the air; people are hugging each other. It's remarkable. We are together. We are Democrats. We didn't concede anything. And we're moving forward.

We're going to bring the fracking vote out. We're going to propose a plan to John Podesta and the Clinton campaign to ban fracking. And we're going to move forward. This is politics. This is how the hot dogs get made. It's an incredible moment in life. We all go out and celebrate.

The entire thing is on C-SPAN. You can watch it if you don't believe me.

The next week, Hillary Clinton comes out, after the platform is ratified, and says she prefers a twelve-dollar-an-hour minimum wage. Noticeably breaking with her own party's platform. The following week, she does a $650,000 fund-raiser with Cheniere Energy, the number-one fracking export company in America. And to top it all off, she appoints Ken Salazar, a known proponent of fracking, as the head of her transition team, a clear slap in the face to a movement that was just getting ready to start supporting her. And we all thought, "What is the point? Was Orlando just a fever dream? You're running against your own party's platform." Ripples went through the electorate. We could feel them.

NO MORE HOT DOGS

It is 3 a.m. It somehow always manages to be 3 a.m.

Once again, I've been driving late into the night. This time to the Democratic Convention in Philly. And once again I pass through that no-man's-land spot, somewhere in Maryland, Delaware,

South Jersey. I pull off, seeing the phantom highway
sign for the Midway Motel. The roof is still partially
blown off, some of the windows still broken, four years
later. A spray-painted plywood board hangs in front,
says "OUT OF BUSINESS."

No more hot dogs.

No more hiccups.

No more sign over the front door that simply says
"YES."

American owned and operated no more.

Abandoned.

In 2016, the American economy had failed the
people. Yes, the press told us that there was a recovery
after the 2008 financial collapse. But in truth, 95
percent of that recovery under Barack Obama had
gone to the 1 percent. That meant that the majority of
the American people were doing the same as or worse
than they had during the 2008 economic collapse. It
also meant that the rich got richer.

That's not a recovery. That's trickle-UP economics.

Maybe that's what happened to the Midway Motel.

ALL THOSE TRUTHS, INALIENABLE

We arrive in Philly to the Democratic
Convention, more divided than ever.

I look out at that huge Wells Fargo
arena in Philly, twenty-five thousand
people. All the states arrayed in the

of tenaciousness and aspiration in America. But it is not a happy room.

As I look out, there are protests breaking out across all the delegations. California's votes have not been counted yet. Bernie delegates from Michigan and Wisconsin and Vermont, Florida, all across the arena, you can see them. Like this giant ocean of humanity, roiling, arguing, divided. Anti-TPP signs. Anti-fracking signs.

Everybody has their truth that they won't compromise. In the same way that I know we can't have three hundred fracked-gas power plants, there are things that they know. They all know their truth. Maybe their brother needs an operation and can't afford it under Obamacare. Maybe it's the fact they are working three jobs and just need one that actually pays fifteen dollars per hour and not twelve. Maybe it's the fact that they have a brother or sister who died in Iraq and they can't vote for someone who sent them overseas. Maybe it's a relative, or five, or ten, from black families put in jail for minor marijuana offenses and they are still rotting in jail twenty years later because of the last Clinton administration's crime bill. Or maybe it's all the factories in the Midwest that have closed—in Wisconsin, Michigan, Pennsylvania, Ohio. Those jobs exported overseas because of NAFTA, written by Bill Clinton. All those truths inalienable!

This was the national stage! It was the place to speak out. For truth and justice.

And when Bernie Sanders did his final act of nominating Hillary Clinton for president himself—a beautiful gesture, but half the room walked out. They stormed the pressroom screaming that they'd been silenced. That their votes had not been counted during the primaries. And that those on the stage were oligarchs and not representative of who they were as Americans. Nobody needed to burn it down at that point. It was already on fire.

THE EARTH IS FLAT

Every night the convention poured out into the bars of Philadelphia. This was not our finest hour, to be honest as a progressive. Drunk, fragmented, and wacko. Delegate voices wake me and I drowned. RURAURAURAURAURA
People are running up to me

RURAURAURAURAURA
saying, We've got incontrovertible proof that the
primaries were stolen in California
RURAURAURAURAURA
There's a clear discrepancy between the exit polls
and the actual votes.
RURAURAURAURAURA
You have to vote for Jill Stein; how can you possibly
vote for a person who is pro-fracking
RURAURAURAURAURA
Warmonger warmonger!!!
RURAURAURAURAURA
Bernie could still get the nomination; this is my
mathematical formula—
RURAURAURAURAURA
It's desperate and it's bonkers.

I remember once, Dr. Cornel West came up to me
and said, "Josh, you know, one out of every six members
of the Black Panther Party was working directly for the
CIA." So I'm thinking there have to be spies. There have
to be infiltrators. So I am counting the people in the bar.
I am going 1, 2, 3, 4, 5, 6, 7, 8, 9, 10, 11, 12, 13 . . . Which
six people in this room are spies?

And a couple of whiskeys in—it's clear that there
are twenty Jill Stein surrogates trying to win over
Bernie folks! I'm having none of this. And I'm telling them the honest truth—she was at a dinner with
Vladimir Putin in Russia, with Julian Assange's father
and Michael Flynn, and she has holdings in Exxon, in

Shell, in Chevron, and $100,000 of stock in DISNEY! How can you be the presidential candidate of the so-called Green Party and not even divest your own money from the fossil fuel industry? She's a fraud! And this guy is fired up and he starts coming after me; and he's got a cameraman with him. He wants to get me on tape in a fistfight in a bar at 3 a.m.! So I run and flee to the opposite side of the bar, I'm trying to find Nomi . . .

Then I get cornered by a person, let's just call him the "handler," you know, a person who handles things for celebrities and influencers; and this *handler* handles some pretty influential and powerful people in progressive politics. So the handler comes up to me, and he's had a couple of whiskeys, and so have I, and he goes,

"Well, you know, I mean, *you know* that the moon landing was faked."

"Moon landing?"

"I mean, *you know*, it was directed by Stanley Kubrick. There was a gap in between *2001* and *A Clockwork Orange* . . ."

"Stanley Kubrick?" I say.

"I mean, come on. Everybody knows this." And he just goes, "And it's very well known in Washington, DC, that there are pedophile circles, and that in those pedophile circles, you know, the code word for young boys is 'pizza.' John Podesta is ordering a lot of pizza."

"John Podesta is a pedophile?????"

He says:

"IT'S COMING. IT'S COMING. DON'T YOU WORRY. YOU'LL SEE."

And then the cohort of the handler, she's a little person, short, wearing a flak vest, camo-cargo shorts, like she's going to war in Bermuda, she's tugging at the handler's sleeve. Saying, "He's here! He's here! I gotta go talk to him."

"Who's here?"

"The 'astronaut.'"

Sure enough, in walks a bona fide astronaut—

And she pulls me over and says:

"He's never been to *space*. We all know that the earth is flat."

"And the North Pole is in the middle. Which is why you always fly over the North Pole to get to Asia, and why you fly over the North Pole to get to Europe. Antarctica doesn't exist. Antarctica is just the perimeter. Have you noticed that you cannot take a flight from Santiago, Chile, to Samoa?"

Actually, I had noticed that.

And I said, "Well, but, um, uh . . . How does the sun go down?" I decided to start with some details. And she goes, "Well, it goes behind a mountain." I said, "Well, but okay, how come then, if you're in the Northern Hemisphere you can see a certain set of stars, like Polaris and the Big Dipper, and if you're in the Southern Hemisphere, you can see the Southern Cross. But you can't see the Southern Cross from the Northern Hemisphere, and you can't see the northern stars from the Southern Hemisphere—how about that?"

She goes, "That's a new one. I haven't heard that one before. But I know there's an explanation."

And I said, "Yes, there's an explanation. *The world is round.*"

But, undeterred, she goes up to, she charges up to this astronaut, who is also tipsy, and starts asking him aggressive questions about space. And he's still recuperating—you know, it is true that astronauts' eyeballs get a little squishy, the vitreous humor and the aqueous humor don't respond so well to the lack of gravity up there, and if they're up there for a very long time, they start getting fuzzy eyes; they start getting space blindness. And I'm thinking to myself, "Can you imagine being on a spacecraft to Mars, for five years, and this person is sitting here telling you that John Podesta is a pedophile and you're going blind?!"

I had to get outta there. I am dodging Jill Stein supporters left and right. Just then, Chris Hayes runs up to me, and he goes, "Josh, Josh, Josh. There was no blacklist at MSNBC."

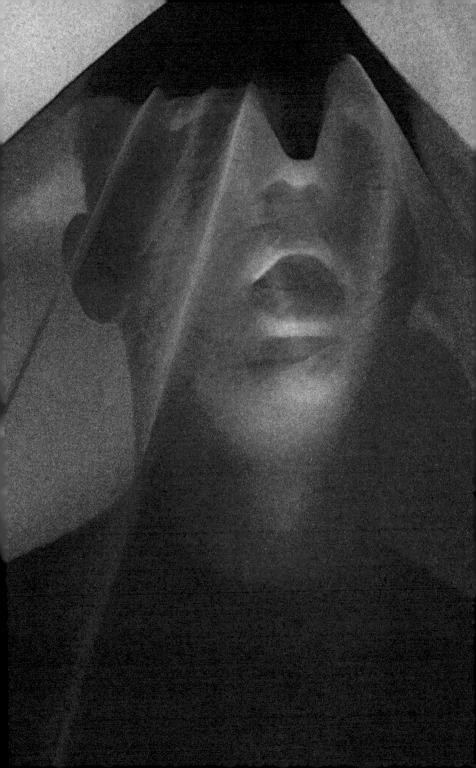

NORMAL LIFE

The shattering and the fragmentation, it was palpable. I just went home. And went to Pennsylvania. I needed to see sunlight break through a line of trees. I needed to feel grass in my fingers. I needed to break the little pieces off the pinecones and smell nature. And at night, I'd go home and think to myself, "How do people believe things that aren't true?" Just on an inkling, on a hunch, I googled "Flat Earth Society and Anti-Semitism." As it turns out, there are videos with tens of millions of views promoting flat Earthism, and then answer videos, and then answer-answer videos, and they're attacking Einstein because he is Jewish, they're all Nazis. Flat Earth Nazis. And science, apparently, is Jewish.

I built a tiny house with my friends and called it the Henry David Thoreau Civil Disobedience Love Shack. I found five kittens in the woods and convinced them to live under my house. You know, normal life.

But normal life had a way of collapsing in 2016. Do you remember I told you about the third guy? The dark shadowy overlord lurking in the rainswept doorway of the propaganda machine? The guy who was working with Breitbart and Phelim McAleer to smear *GASLAND* in 2012?

On August 20, 2016, that guy took over the Trump campaign. He was named Steve Bannon—head of Breitbart.com, bankrolled by a famous hedge-fund billionaire named Robert Mercer, and in August 2016 about to replace Paul Manafort as Donald Trump's campaign manager.

AND Steve Bannon was about to tell you exactly the story you wanted to hear.

Steve Bannon and Robert Mercer were also on the board of an operation called Cambridge Analytica. Cambridge Analytica that you've all been reading about quite a lot recently—

Lemme go back a few thousand years.

The word "democracy" is derived from the Greek *demos*. The *demos* are the people, right? Presumably the educated people that understand facts and science. But let's leave that aside. *Demos*, it's also, you know, the root of the word "demographics." Demographics are really simple, you know, all the things that characterize you: your age, your race, your sex, where you live, how much money you make. Demographics. A lot of campaign information is based on demographics. If you're black, and you're sixty-seven, and you're in North Carolina, you're going to vote a certain way. If you're white, and you're in the Ohio suburbs, and you're thirty-six years old, you're going to vote a certain way. Demographics.

Now the US is getting less white, less rich, and less old. More young people, more people of color. In other words, more people that tend to be progressive. Demographics in America right now overwhelmingly favor Democrats.

So a new way to slice up the electorate was invented.

That's something I discovered, sitting there in the woods. It makes demographics look like fumbling in the dark.

It's called *psycho*-graphics.

SCENE 14

THE OCEAN INSIDE YOU

In 2014, a young grad student from Warsaw named Michal Kosinski and some friends at Cambridge University's Psychometrics Centre made a huge discovery. He could map your precise behavioral psychological profile to Facebook based on what you "liked."

In the field of behavioral psychology, psychometrics are behavioral characteristics that can serve as predictors. Who you really are deep down and how you are going to behave. They are like currents in the ocean; you can see how something or someone is going to flow.

In fact, the acronym for the basic psychological traits that make up every human is OCEAN. O-C-E-A-N. As it turns out, you have an ocean inside you, and it tells us a lot about who you are. *O* for openness. How open are you to new ideas and to the world? *C* for conscientiousness. How meticulous or anal are you? *E* for extroversion. How much do you like people—how outgoing are you? *A*—agreeableness. How considerate are you and cooperative? And *N*, my favorite, neuroticism. How much are you an anxious, worried wreck? These five traits can give us your intimate psychological portrait.

But what Kosinski figured out was he could take behavioral psych data and plot it up against Facebook.

He developed something called the "My Personality App." And just for kicks, just for fun, he got some of his friends to fill these questionnaires out. First a few hundred, but it went viral and hundreds of thousands of people filled them out. Kosinski matched that questionnaire data up against people's Facebook profiles. Facebook told him what kinds of things we liked or didn't like. And Kosinski mapped your OCEAN personality against your Facebook personality. And voilà, he could tell what your psychometric personality was from looking at Facebook alone. You no longer had to divulge your personality secrets. Facebook betrayed them for you. And he started to be able to predict people's future behavior based on that model. He famously said, "If I know 70 of your likes on Facebook, that's enough to outdo what your friends know about you. If I know 150 likes that you clicked on Facebook, I know you better than your parents know you." And at 300 likes, Kosinski intimated, the algorithm knows you better than you know yourself.

The day comes, he publishes his results and he gets two phone calls. A threatened lawsuit and a job offer, he told a German magazine, both of them from Facebook.

Now your personality is in the matrix. You are telling your story to it.

And Google does this, too.

We knew already that Google was targeting certain people in certain areas. It's called addressable-ad technology. But don't forget, Google knows everything you are searching for. What you know, what you don't know, and what you want, on an intimate level. And you buy your quest. With your credit card and all that data, the algorithm is being tipped off to all the things that you personally crave.

How deep is the ocean? What can it predict?

It's a trope in marketing, it goes like this: "If we get them when they're six months old, we have them as customers for life." So Target, the superstore, actually created a program to predict which of its customers were pregnant, to market to them while their off-spring were in utero. The story goes that based on their Google search data Target sent maternity guides to this one house in Michigan, and the father in the house went ballistic. He assaulted his local Target's manager, waving these maternity brochures in the air, saying, "Why are you trying to convince my daughter, who is only seventeen, to have babies?" And a few weeks later, he calls up and says, "I'm so sorry. I didn't realize. She was already pregnant." Target knew this seventeen-year-old was pregnant before her dad did, based on her Google searches.

How deep is the OCEAN? Will it tell you no lies?

What kind of person are you? What kind of Democrat or Republican are you? Well, somehow, Cambridge Analytica got hold of the model, and harvested data from hundreds of millions of people, and started to use it to target specific, political messages to specific people. Do you remember when I got different Google results in Pennsylvania than in New York? This was as if every single person's politics were being revealed by where they were, who they were, and what they were like on the inside.

This is based on you. Every single piece of information filtered through your personal algorithm. Your IP address, your Facebook feed. The men behind the algorithmic curtain can determine what you see and then profoundly influence what you do. And this has developed faster than the speed of morality.

Facebook actually had a way that advertisers could target certain things to certain races. If you were advertising an apartment on Facebook, you could specify that only white people—no black people—could see those posts. Twenty-first-century Jim Crow. And no one would know. Maybe that was the point.

It goes much further than even that. Every single major corporation is amassing this data. So that they can tailor what you see online specifically to you.

There are at least nine companies in America that have and sell this data. Have you heard of these companies?

Corelogic, Datalogix, eBureau, ID Analytics, Intelius, PeekYou, Rapleaf, Acxiom, and Recorded Future. They've heard of you! They know you better than you know yourself. And they're selling your data. Every time you click those terms and conditions, every single time, you're letting them into your Internet DNA.

They're making reports on you all the time. Because, on one level, your cell phone is a constantly evolving, deepening, more and more profound psychological data test that you're filling out all the time. Everywhere you go, everything that you buy, everything that you do, you're leaving psychological tracks. Every one of your movements in the real world *and* the cyber world.

You are a constant cascade of statistics flowing through the machine.

And you are in a box, a category. Are you a "Millennial weekend psychopharmaceutical user?" Or a "Homebound thrifty senior who posts about cats and the environment?" Are you "New Age/organic lifestyle with patchouli on back order from Etsy," or "Biker/ Hell's Angels into '80s TV memorabilia?" "Member of five or more online shopping sites," "people with pellet stoves," "hypochondriacs that book doctor's appointments after doing a lot of medical googling," "those who have credit at a low-end grocery store," "collectors of fetishistic Elvis tchotchkes"?

On and on. Household, race and ethnicity, surname, method of payment, number of orders, loans, financial data, presence of an elderly parent who is over seventy-five, presence of young children in the household with Xboxes, employed, white collar, unemployed, blue collar, work at home.

Three kids in after-school athletics searching for plane tickets to South America alarm set to wake up at 5:30 snoozes three times every morning has two weeks off a year . . .

Early pregnancy termination, watches John McCain speeches, old Marx Brothers movies, texts and googles at the same time, seventeen years old ordering acne medication . . .

Mole removed from left side, speaks Chinese, fender bender 9:45 p.m., types sixty words a minute, skin cancer screening in three weeks, reads Danielle Steel and *The Da Vinci Code* . . .

Searched cul-de-sac, Amy Schumer, Chuck Schumer, Sasha Grey, pinot noir discounts, stays

up late looking at pictures of homemade aircraft,
Connecticut, $66K a year . . .

Buys toilet paper online and lesbian S and M porn
while searching eHarmony for extramarital affairs.
We know you. We know you. Heavy whiskey drinker,
donates to animal rights causes late at night, watches
penis enlargement videos, assault rifles, drives a '99
Hyundai, sexts with coworkers, four kids, divorced,
pro-fracking Kasich voter, leaves the house at 1 a.m.
to go to the strip club on Route 97 three to four times
a week, lost ten teeth to infection, twenty-three, one
credit short of college graduation, purchased yoga pants
and yoga mats, googles yoga classes but doesn't sign up,
two cats named Stanley and Blanche, underweight, on
Tinder, studio apartment, waxes legs, texts over one
hundred times a day, hair products, $16K a year.

We know you, we know you. We know what you
dream about doing, we know what your sexual fanta-
sies and insecurities are, we know your biases, we know
your insides. What you think you are doing in private
you are doing in front of all of us, all the time. All
the things you regret. All the things you are proud of.
What you post, what you promote, what you believe.
We know you. We know you so well.

We spend all our time obsessing about you.
Perfecting your personal algorithm to sell you to the
highest bidder.

You're not just 70 percent water and tissue and a bag
of bones, you're an open ocean of information.

The data swarms and dives like Niagara Falls.

Cambridge Analytica has amassed four to five thousand data points on every adult American.

And Alexander Nix, the head of Cambridge Analytica, famously came out, just a few weeks before the election, and announced that Donald Trump was using their services. Trump canvassers in Michigan and Wisconsin would go from household to household. Now, they didn't just know your political leanings or party affiliation. The app told them who you were psychologically, with suggestions on how to tailor the conversation to the personality types of their target voters. Real, live addressable-ad tech. The app told them who you are, not just demographically—psycho-graphically. Trump and Cambridge Analytica knew you better than you knew yourself.

The demographic river that is flowing toward the Democrats—dammed and rerouted.

So on Facebook they could target ads against Hillary Clinton specifically pointed at black men only, and no one else would see them playing up that Hillary was a racist. Facebook even created a specific search pegged to the words "Jew hater." But unless you searched for or were a Jew hater you couldn't see it. These are called "dark posts." And they could manipulate your Google searches.

Don't like that? Too bad. The Internet is doing that to you every day. Four to five thousand data points on every American.

The Internet knows your sickness, but it doesn't give you a cure. A collective cure. It gives your disease right back to you. Like an addiction, you get your mirror, falling toward you.

In fact, in the future, most newspaper articles will be written by machines. AI is already writing a lot of what you see in the newspaper. But it will be cheaper for AI to write five thousand stories that go to five thousand subscribers than for a publisher to pay one journalist who can write one that's actually true. It will say something like, "You remember that it was cloudy on the day of your graduation, well, the Trump administration is facing similar storms this week . . ." That kind of thing. FAKE NEWS FOR YOU! FAKE NEWS FOR YOU! EVERYBODY GETS FAKE NEWS! A fake story for every "real" you!

CLIMATE CHANGE IS A HOAX! John Podesta likes to have sex with young boys and code word "pizza"! Or *GASLAND* is a LIE and EVERYTHING JOSH FOX SAYS IS UNTRUE.

In certain places on the Internet, that IS what is true.

You won't find the *New York Times* or *Washington Post*, actual journalism, until page four of your Google search. Buried wayyyyy down at the bottom. Real journalism sunk with an algorithmic Corexit to the bottom of the feed.

This is the balkanization of truth.

The psycho-crats have taken over.

But when Alexander Nix announced that he was helping Trump, he also said something that has implications far, far beyond any one election, any one political moment. He announced that in the future, our children will not understand the concept of mass marketing/mass communication. No more universal stories, you know? Every piece of data is going to be specifically targeted at you.

In the future, each of you will get your own slogan.

No more, as Shakespeare wrote about the theater, "all our minds transfigured so together."

This is the new narrative. You get you, over and over again. Like the corporation speaking to you out of the mirror.

And let me tell you, the truth here is that *we* did this to us. This was Facebook, this was Google, this was American. And there is nothing that the "Russians bots" did that multinational oil companies haven't been doing for more than a decade. We created a universe in which your truth is yours only. Steve Bannon, Robert Mercer, Americans.

You see only what they want you to see, which is what *you* want you to see. You are perpetually stuck up there at three thousand feet, the oil and toxicity floating on the OCEAN just looks like pretty sunshine lapping at the waves. You can't see the toxicity.

You see, 9/11 was a shared event. It happened to all of us.

These people know YOUR 9/11, whatever it is. They

know if that girl rejected you in the eighth grade. They know if you're an angry white man, or a neurotic Asian woman. They know your wounds. They know your trauma. They know your scars.

They're counting them. And they tailor that message to your vulnerability exclusively.

So what Steve Bannon and Andrew Breitbart did to me when I toured *GASLAND*, Cambridge Analytica, through Google and Facebook, figured out how to do to 200 million people. A smear campaign against reality itself.

I know, I was one of their beta tests. Look what they are doing to the Parkland kids now.

No longer the crude, costly method of tailing a single person around the country. Now they could get your intimate details, group them, advertise to them. It is as if they are following you around. Following millions of people around. Harassing your psyche. Learning your weaknesses, putting you through the wringer. A fear campaign aimed at everyone and every-thing, the fears that can push the electorate to where they want it to go.

Climb. Climb. Climb.

The Industrial Age left 150 years of pollution in the ground and centuries of CO_2 and methane in the atmosphere. Pools of toxic chemicals in the actual earth, underneath the crust. To take all of that toxicity out, 150 years' worth of toxicity, is probably going to be impossible.

But, you see, this is another level of pollution. Digital pollution. Toxic data everywhere. Remember that guy who drove all the way from North Carolina with an AR-15 and burst into the pizza place and shot it up, yelling, "Where are the kids?!" That's the toxic cyber world invading the real world.

The cyber world is its own cyber truth. It may not have any relationship to analog truth. That's a world where climate change really doesn't exist. It's a whole planet on which science is irrelevant.

And when the truth is lost in the cyberstorm, the men behind the algorithmic curtain get what they want. And right now, they're winning.

First it was the election in Kenya in 2013. Then the Ukraine in 2014. Then Brexit. Then Mexican elections, Brazil impeachment, Malaysian and Australian elections. Cambridge Analytica's hands across the world. And then, in that wilderness of mirrors, that haze when all of our individual truths pushed us into different corners of reality, America elects a racist, authoritarian, anti-science, climate-change-denying Cheeto.

And yes, one Saturday night at the stroke of midnight, Facebook, in the ultimate gesture of shutting the barn doors after the horses have run away, banned Cambridge Analytica.

But what you didn't read in the *New York Times* is that Cambridge Analytica has had a contract with the State Department since March 2017. A year. The objective: to influence elections in dozens of countries around the world. A year's worth of psychographic training.

Is Facebook going to kick out the State Department?

Then, in March 2018, Cambridge Analytica announced to the world that they were bankrupt and closing their doors. In the same month, however, practically the exact same board of directors and investors formed a brand-new company with the same mission. Emerdata.

Because long after the theatrics and the bad acting of Zuckerberg and Congress, these tools of influence will remain. They're like the bomb. Part of our lives now. Of course, they want you to forget about them. They're more effective that way.

Presidents may come and go, but the data is unimpeachable.

How do you know what's true? How can you differentiate between a progressive-sounding Russian troll saying, "You're using Russians to avoid looking at America," from a progressive-sounding American troll saying, "You're using Russians to avoid looking at America"?

And who gets paid better per hour? Isn't that the whole American dream right there? Hope looking out on the horizon? And now, our heads forced down, staring, like Narcissus, at our own reflections in the palm-sized liquid crystal pools where we drown.

SCENE 15

GLACIERS

Right after the election, I went to
Iceland. I drove out to the glaciers. You
could watch them melting. You could
see this march of little icebergs off to
the ocean. Some of the tours up the
glacier had been canceled because a
couple of SUVs had dropped through

109

in places where the ice was thinner than they thought. And the people were lost. Just gone. No idea where they went. Disappeared. Inside some underground river, inside the glacier. All the white and blue ice in sheaves. The people didn't know what hit them.

And as I was walking down the street in Reykjavik, the newspaper headline struck me like a thunderbolt.

"Rex Tillerson"—that doughy, dimpled denier, CEO of ExxonMobil—"Nominated for Secretary of State"—Hillary's old job.

I lay down on a snowbank like a snow angel at the edge of the embankment, my head hanging over the edge so I could look out at the bay, my chin toward the sky. I could see the world upside down. The floating glaciers looked like clouds passing by overhead, the ocean was the sky, and the sky was beneath my feet.

Upside down, I pieced it all together. My life, the arc of this story, the world. The information was all there, but it was all backward. You had to see it upside down to really see it.

I was never gonna escape fracking. Not even all the way up in the Arctic.

And the Arctic wasn't gonna escape it either.

And the doughy, dimpled denier and the bearbaiting Bond villain hatched a plan, as archvillains always do, to end the world.

I'm pretty sure most of you have seen the pictures.

When they were having a champagne toast together in 2012, Rex Tillerson, who was then the head of

ExxonMobil, had struck a $500 billion deal with
Rosneft, the Russian state oil company, to frack and
drill in the Arctic Circle.

A huge partnership between the largest oil companies
in the world, to drill in uncharted territory. The Arctic
had melted enough to get oil rigs to the top of the world.
Russia and Exxon's bid for another century of oil.

But something funny had happened on the way to
their big payoff.

The anti-fracking movement exploded in Europe.
We toured and organized and got fracking banned in
France, Germany, Italy, Poland, Romania, Bulgaria,
the Netherlands, Scotland, Ireland—virtually the
whole continent.

And Barack Obama and Hillary Clinton were pushing fracking in all those places. Why? As a check on
Russian power.

Russia supplies Europe with most of its natural gas.

So Hillary and Barack, arm in arm with the frackers, went to compete. American fracking! Instead of
pushing renewable energy, which could power all of
Europe, American fracking tech would liberate Europe
from that bear-baiting Bond villain.

And our movement got in the way. Then events in
Ukraine happened.

In 2014, thanks to Hillary and Obama, the
pro-fracking president of the Ukraine, Viktor
Yanukovych, signs two multibillion-dollar deals with
Shell and Chevron to frack the Ukraine. But then

the people play a hand, and a popular uprising in the Ukraine manages to unseat Yanukovych. A victory for the people and their burgeoning anti-fracking movement. But then Yanukovych flees to Russia, where he convinces Vladimir Putin to invade and take over. Putin invades the Ukraine, overthrowing the people. Barack Obama and Hillary Clinton push back—they impose sanctions against Russia for invading. The sanctions kill the Exxon deal. ExxonMobil and Rosneft's big, big payoff, canceled. And sanctions against Russia also prevent any American fracking technology from being deployed in the Ukraine. Major bummer for Exxon. Major bummer for Putin.

But now with Trump as president, Rex Tillerson, head of Exxon, becomes our secretary of state.

Never before was the George Carlin joke more true, that America is an oil company with an army.

ExxonMobil, the biggest fracking company in the world, climate-change deniers, and the number-one fracking company in the world, now running all of US diplomacy.

Tillerson and Steven Mnuchin, through presidential executive order, are now in charge of US sanctions policy against Russia. They appeal to try to get the sanctions lifted. It causes an outrage in the midst of the Russian investigation. ExxonMobil is fined $4 million for trying to disrupt the sanctions. They back off. In fact, just a few weeks after that, they back all the way the fuck off. In March 2018 Exxon Mobil officially ends its Arctic dealings with Rosneft. And, predictably, two weeks later, Rex Tillerson is fired as secretary of state by Donald Trump via tweet.

Head spinning yet? Next, it is announced that Rex Tillerson, of ExxonMobil, is to be replaced by Mike Pompeo, the congressman who took more money from one of ExxonMobil's chief rivals—i.e., the Koch brothers—than any congressman in history. A climate-change denier. And the Kochs announce that they plan to spend a record-breaking $400 million on the midterm elections.

And in the same month that ExxonMobil announces that the Rosneft deal is off, pulling out $3.5 billion in investment in the Russian Arctic—what do they do? They announce that they're going to invest $50 billion in fracking America. In Texas. The Gulf of Mexico. New Mexico. Louisiana. Can't drill the Arctic? Might as well frack America.

But not to be outdone, Ryan Zinke, our interior secretary, and Donald Trump open up offshore drilling on 100 percent of America's coastlines. The Atlantic, the Pacific, and, crucially, Alaska, in the Arctic.

Shortly thereafter, Vladimir Putin and Rosneft announce that they have a new partner to drill in the Arctic: BP.

So all this has set off an international Cold War–style race. Not an arms race. A race to drill.

That's what I saw there upside down in melting-Ice-land.

Underneath all of this—9/11, the Iraq War, fracking in America, *Deepwater Horizon*, Hillary and Obama's push of fracking around the world—every last piece of this, underneath it, is oil, oil, oil.

And the white supremacists who control it believe they can blow up everyone and everything in the world to stay in power. Instead of renewable energy, which can power everything and empower everyone on earth.

And Nazis are marching on the streets of America in 2018.

The hidden trauma of the earth, the marrowbone, the remnants of the last mass extinction being dug up to bring the new mass extinction.

That is when it clicked for me.

It's totally legal for Exxon to tamper in our elections. And legal for them to tamper with the climate.

Because they are in charge. We don't live in a democracy. We live in an oil-igarchy.

It's like a merry-go-round. Rex Tillerson gets off, Mike Pompeo gets on. ExxonMobil gets off, BP gets on. Vladimir Putin comes in, Donald Trump gets off. Theresa May gets on. It's a coterie of oligarchs on a carousel. And democracy, the planet, our climate, and quite possibly the species, is getting lost in the funhouse mirrors surrounding it all.

Which came first, the president or the secretary of state?

Trump didn't pick Tillerson and the oil industry. The oil industry picked Trump, then picked Rex, then . . .

The oil industry seems to be picking them all.

What is the difference between a Russian oil oligarch saying there was no interference in the elections and an American oil oligarch saying there was no interference in the elections?

You're right about the Russians.

You're right about the oil industry.

They are the same people.

Putin already has control over his oil company and his state and his elections.

And it is clear that the oil industry just wants the same deal in America.

It is not a magic trick. Rex Tillerson didn't simply emerge from a field of qualified applicants.

They could have picked whatever office they wanted.

The oil companies are choosing the president.

Both pollutions are coming together. The physically toxic and the cybernetically toxic.

It is not that Vladimir Putin was "interfering" in our election. It is that oil companies are getting together and making deals and governments are getting in the way. Democracies get in the way.

I had assumed that Obama was battling with Putin and using natural gas resources as leverage in that battle.

But isn't it more that natural gas resources were battling for territories and using Obama and Putin in ways that reflect those interests which are far more powerful?

And one other thing seemed abundantly clear.

The people want a revolution. I saw it.

So you've gotta control their brains.

You've gotta fragment and divide and conquer and psycho-psych it out.

Because our truths support each other.

We want the white suburban insomniac soccer mom who googles fracking chemicals and the black urban fast-food worker on the front lines of the fight for $15 and the Nuyorican veteran trying to get off OxyContin for his PTSD and the white kid who survived the Parkland shooting and the black kid who survived the last police shooting. The scientist and the poet. We want them in the same room. We want the collective. We want unity and we can achieve it if we know the system we are in.

But it is the oil interests that want to divide you with your data to drive your SUV crashing through the ice.

The ant isn't suicidal.

The microbe isn't either.

It's using the ant.

Driving itself toward an evolutionary conclusion.

The microbe wants to reproduce.

Just as the oil companies drive the governments to have their paradigm continue.

People want a revolution.

A peaceful, political revolution.

That is why we are being cordoned off onto our psycho-suicidal blades of grass.

And there on the Icelandic shore, staring upside down at the sky of ocean, the mirror flips. My mirror self dove out of the ocean and up into a melting sky.

The truth was growing wings.

And while we're watching the merry-go-round of the investigations go round and round and tuning into ourselves again and again at the top of our news feeds, Donald Trump's administration has rescinded all climate and clean energy goals and a total of sixty-seven environmental rules have been—or are about to be— rescinded, including regulations on methane emissions and reporting.

Steve Bannon wasn't doing election interference in 2012.

He was working to promote fracking. And deny climate change—he was working for the oil companies.

He never stopped.

And he has always been a Nazi.

The atmosphere of the earth is 5 percent wetter. Wet, hot, humid air. And that has upset the balance of how every drop of water flows and moves around this planet. And the Internet—I don't know—20, 50 percent, 75 percent untrue. And that has changed the way all of our collective reality moves. And all of our collective politics. And, of course, everybody is going to be coming after you, whether it's Breitbart, Steve Bannon and Cambridge Analytica, or the troll farms in the Ukraine and in Russia.

Weaponized data is here to stay and it is coming for you.

Because for the very first time in history, big data has become the most valuable resource on earth. As big as oil, or bigger. Both forms of toxicity driving each other, the actual and the cyber.

Welcome to Cold War 2.0 and hot warming earth three degrees.

Do you feel it?

The impulse to climb and be eaten? Isolated from it. All alone.

Without a collective notion of truth, of shared beliefs, of science, of the story that we're all telling ourselves and each other, without a sense of collective verification. We're all on our own little planets. Not in a theater all assembled together. But on our own little suicidal blades of grass.

SCENE 16

STANDING ROCK

Where was the collective? Where was our
collective soul?
   I found it.
   The first people of this land, a cry
emerging from the center of this continent.
   I'm talking about Standing Rock,
North Dakota.

A new revolt in the name of water and justice had been born: the Water Protectors—a band of twenty thousand people from all across the world, young and old, from all races but led by the indigenous people from Standing Rock, assembled at the bend of the Cannonball River to stop a fracked-oil pipeline, the Dakota Access Pipeline, from running underneath the Missouri River, or Mni Sose—the tribe's only source of water and the headwaters for eighteen million people's drinking water downstream.

Five hundred years of colonialism and racism on display acting on behalf of big oil.

I walk up and see the face-off, about thirty or so young Water Protectors, standing waist-deep in the freezing Cannonball River, at the bank of Turtle Island, the sacred burial ground for the tribe. A line of a hundred or so police in full riot gear blocking them from coming onshore. The Water Protectors, vulnerable and praying. "We love you!" they say to the police. "We are here fighting for your children's water. Please leave our sacred burial grounds. All we want is clean water." Innocent, calm, and peaceful, they plead. Then, the whole line—BOOM!—is maced. Rubber bullets shot.

I felt as if I were witnessing a dying empire. I felt like I was watching the salt mine protests of Gandhi, where hundreds of Indians allowed themselves to be clubbed, beaten, and killed in protest against the abuses of the British Empire.

North Dakota police had been destroying sacred

objects, eagle feathers stripped off religious leaders, peace pipes broken. During an October 22 raid, tribe members were ripped out of sweat lodges and arrested in the middle of religious ceremonies. Teepee flaps opened up with the muzzle end of M-4 rifles.

And yet at the front lines they say, "All we want is clean water." One of the protectors says to the police, "What will you do when you wake up in the middle of the night and your child asks you for a glass of water? Will you say that you were standing here with us, protecting this vital source of life? Or will you tell your child that you had a gun to my head?"

On the day that we call Thanksgiving—you know, the original fake news?—the Water Protectors were building a bridge to go to the other side of the river, where they could pray to their ancestors. The police were up on the hill with water cannons, shooting freezing water down. Some of the Protectors described being attacked by weaponized water as a kind of rape. And the police are looking down, and they're saying, "Do not build the bridge. Do not cross the bridge. We do not want to have a confrontation with you *today*." As if somehow saying, "Don't you know what day it is? We can't have a fight with Native Americans on Thanksgiving."

But here it is with plywood and weird sheets of insulation. And they're hitting it with rusty hammers, and ax handles, and tying it together with rope, and I'm thinking, "This cannot possibly work. There's no way this bridge is going to get eighty feet across the

Cannonball River to the other side. How is this going to happen?"

And I'm moving back and forth through the crowd, everywhere, and there's mud and you can see people's breath and the drums are going and police are up on the ridge with M-4 rifles and they have orange shotguns to shoot the rubber bullets out of. On the side is the Orwellian inscription "Less Lethal." Only 2 percent who get shot with rubber bullets actually die. So they're *less lethal*. I go back into the crowd and there's Shailene Woodley, and she's got only her eyes visible; she's got a huge parka on. She gives me a big hug and she says, "Josh, the elders are saying anyone who crosses that bridge today could lose their life."

And we're well aware. Just two or three nights before, police had hurled concussion grenades into the crowd, blowing off the arm of Sophia Wilansky, a twenty-one-year-old Water Protector from the Bronx. She was losing her arm and was in the ICU in Minneapolis. And we know for certain if it had hit her in the chest, or hit her in the neck, or hit her in the head, there's absolutely no way she would've survived.

I start back and see—the bridge is working! It's floating! And hundreds of people start to cross to pray. Nonviolent and saying, "Stay in prayer mode. Don't over-react. Don't show the police any violence or any anger."

At the foot of the bridge they say, "Here's cedar. Put this cedar in your shoe. It's going to protect you." As I walked across, bathed in sage smoke, I said, "If I get my leg blown off, I'll become a one-legged dancer. If I get my arm blown off, I'll become a one-armed banjo player. And if I die, I die here among friends." That kind of love, it surrounds you and envelops you. It protects you.

I don't really know much about prayer. I never really participated in that kind of thing. I do know that people who are projecting their most peaceful selves out in front of them and who are concentrating on being peaceful and clear have an enormous amount of power. These people were fighting for everyone on the planet.

And we are lucky that day. The police don't shoot. The Protectors hold their ceremony. Floris White Bull tells me, "It makes our ancestors proud to be here in prayer. Thanksgiving Day was actually a massacre. That's the real story. We call it Survivors' Day."

SWEAT LODGE EARTH

That night, I'm invited to go to a sweat lodge ceremony with Doug Goodfeather, one of the great-grandnephews of Sitting Bull.

I arrive there at dusk; a fire has been burning for five hours near the opening of the lodge, and at the bottom of the fire are the lava rocks, probably six or

seven dozen rocks. They call these rocks the grandfathers. They heat up so hot they are white hot and
pink hot. We all file in and I guess there's a lot of
PTSD to go around on this day. Everybody wants
to sweat with Doug Goodfeather. The sweat lodge
is a small dome; maybe twelve feet in diameter and
about four feet high, the floor is the earth. You have
to crawl through the flap. When they close that flap
door it is absolutely 100 percent pitch black. You
cannot see a thing. Doug opens the flap and tells the
fire keeper, "Bring in the grandfathers. Bring in ten
grandfathers." They bring ten pink-hot rocks, using
antlers to move them to the center. Goodfeather
sprinkles bear root and cedar root on it. It's a sweet,
antiseptic smell. You're half-naked in your boxer
shorts with a towel around your neck and someone's
knee is in your back and there is a foot over here and
it is so totally cramped and incredibly uncomfortable and he says, "You know, this type of suffering
teaches us compassion. Death teaches us how to cry.
Suffering teaches us how to pray." He talked about
how he lost his daughter to leukemia when she was
pregnant and he had two tours of duty in Iraq and
he didn't want to live. These ceremonies brought
him back from the dead.

Here comes the first splash of that *mni wiconi*,
that water of life. He throws a splash of water onto
the grandfathers and you can see that glow just
extinguish and then KSHHHHH! This incredible

steam in the air. This billowing steam. It's hotter than you've ever felt. It's 20 degrees outside and now it's 120 inside that sweat lodge. So hot that I instantaneously got a burn on the front of my nose. I got a burn on the back of my ears. You're gasping for air, the air is so thick with water. There's so much water in the air that you don't know what to do and KSHHH! KSHH!! They're pounding on the drums and they're singing and they're pounding and it's like voices coming from far far far away. You've never heard songs like this. You have no idea where they're coming from. All the people seem to know the words. I have no idea how long this goes on, an hour? Three hours? I've lost all bearings.

And then, out of this mist, in the total darkness, I see my grandfather. The Italian who committed suicide. I've never met him. I've never thought to ask him anything before. And he simply says, "I'm sorry. Forgive me." He says, "I saw too much. But I died to make room for you, as all men do. Die to make room for what comes next. What will come next, we don't know."

I'm sobbing. I'm weeping. I can't breathe. I can't catch my breath. I open my eyes— darkness. I close my eyes—darkness.

The eye wall of the hurricane approaches at 180 miles an hour.

Inside the storm, shards of metal roof dance like shrapnel.

Seas roiling and boiling and surging.
Buildings imploding with water and fire.
I'm floating on bodies.
Arms and legs.
An ocean of people.
A great rising tide
holding me up
But are they
drowning or are they marching?
Are they submerged or are they
rising? Flying high up up up.
A human wave.
All around me
Screams of agony and shouts of joy.
A vision.
A prophecy?
I see it.

Floodwaters are certain, icy and rushing in fast,
they overtake your furniture, your windows,
and, finally, you.
Will we go down to breathe that last breath?

Cities drowned, streets submerged?
The carbon dioxide and methane invisibly
heating up the earth, like hot breath inside
a plastic bag, the bloated exhalings of all of
our industrial processes, the sky swollen and
angry—a rage building storms on rumbling
oceans . . .

And underneath all of it, a belligerent, predatory program, a digital microbe, a pathogen seeking out our most hidden desires and wounds, forcing us in the dark toward extinction.

I'm trying to break its logic.

I'm trying to hold my breath.

I'm trying to think of something that I cannot possibly conceive.

And suddenly I know. I know why the hiccup cure works.

The hiccup cure works because you're holding your breath, and your life is threatened. Just for a few seconds, your life is totally—if you don't breathe again, you're going to die. And then there's this thought that breaks your brain. Thinking of something that can't possibly exist, not even in your own mind. It draws you out of what you're stuck in, the broken record. The hiccup is your fear; the groove that keeps skipping, back and forth—paralyzed. Your life is being threatened and your brain is absorbing something bigger than it can possibly conceive. That is climate change. That is the cyber world. How could you possibly conceive of every ecological system on the planet? All of those intricacies, all of those things. Only a computer can see those climate models. The cyber world is infinitely complex. It's a thousand, million, billion, trillion interactions. Can you see it?

The truth has changed.

We are the first generation to know with absolute scientific certainty what the global apocalypse will look like.

That means we have a choice.

It's the ant that doesn't climb, that evolves. Freaks of Darwinian natural selection are how evolution happens. Usually across millions of years, not decades. But for humans, evolution does not have to be random. It is a choice.

We can break the cycle.

KSSSSHHHHHHHHHHH!!!!

The wind picks up. The water in the air forms into a violent swirl.

All of a sudden I'm back in the bathtub during Hurricane Sandy.

I'm cowering for cover.

The roof explodes off the Midway Motel.

I see the water in the air like changing algorithms, spiraling patterns, like another planet is being born, a paradigm shift.

I fly up into it. Up, up, up, up.

I see the ocean from a terrific height, beckoning.
The great surge is coming in.
What will we see there? Inside all that water?

Music begins as Josh lifts off from his desk, flying up. The mysterious melody of Alex Ebert's "Truth" echoes through the theater. As Josh ascends, the ceiling comes off the roof of the Midway Motel, revealing stars and swirling clouds and mist. Josh dances high above the stage, twirling and diving and floating. A projected chalk outline of himself falls down away from him, he watches it go. He dances as the song continues.

Blackout.